Sir Francis Drake

Around the oval portrait: · 1598 · ✠ FRANCISCVS DRACO NOBILISSIMVS ANGLIAE EQVES, REI NAVTICAE AC BELLICAE PERITISSIMVS

AVDENTES FORTV-
NA IVVAT

Cognita Nasoni mea si quoque vita fuisset,
Neptuni verè sobolem narrasset, et alis
Expansis Mundum circumuolitasse per vndas,
Flammiuom in mira metamorphosi vsque Draconem
Conuersum fueram semper sic faucibus ipse,
Vnguibus atque alis, caudáq; armatus in hostem .

SIR FRANCIS DRAKE

*An Exhibition to Commemorate
Francis Drake's Voyage
around the World
1577 - 1580*

Published for
THE BRITISH LIBRARY
by
BRITISH MUSEUM PUBLICATIONS LIMITED

ISBN 0 7141 0393 4

Published by
British Museum Publications Ltd.,
6 Bedford Square, London WC1B 3RA

British Library Cataloguing in Publication Data

British Library
  Sir Francis Drake.
  1. Drake, *Sir* Francis   2. British Library
  3. Voyages around the world
  910'.41   C420.D7

Designed by John Mitchell
Printed in Great Britain by
Balding & Mansell Ltd., London and Wisbech

Contents

Abbreviations

B.M.   British Museum
B.N.   Bibliothèque Nationale
P.R.O.   Public Record Office
PROB 11 . . . Prerogative Court of Canterbury
          registered copy wills.
SP 12   . . . State Papers Domestic, Reign of
          Elizabeth I
SP 94   . . . State Papers Foreign (Spain),
          1577–1780.

Introduction

'HIS name was a terrour to the French, Spaniard, Portugal, and Indians. Many Princes of Italy, Germany, and others, as well enemies as friends in his life time desired his Picture. He was the second that ever went through the Straights of Magellan . . . in briefe he was famous in Europe, and America, as Tamburlaine in Asia, and Affrica. In his imperfections hee was ambitious for honor, unconstant in amity, greatly affected to popularity.' Thus the early seventeenth century chronicler, Edmund Howes, in his *Chronicles* of 1615, provided a fitting assessment of Sir Francis Drake.

The popular hero of the anti-Spanish cause in England, Francis Drake pursued a career common enough among Elizabethan seamen, that of privateering. His success as a privateer was spectacular. In 1577 he set out on a voyage through the Strait of Magellan into the Pacific Ocean where he intended to plunder the unsuspecting ships and ports of the Spanish South American empire. In the course of the navigation he discovered that Tierra del Fuego bounding the Strait to the south was not part of the southern continent as hitherto believed, but an archipelago. He thus revealed the possibility of a navigable passage south of Tierra del Fuego, the route to be discovered in 1616 round Cape Horn. Along the coasts of Chile, Peru and Mexico he attacked Spanish ports and captured some forty ships, including the 'Cacafuego', laden with bullion which, when weighed officially on his return, amounted to over ten tons, enough to defray 'the charge of seaven yeeres Warres, prevent, and save the Common Subject from Taxes, Loans [*etc.*] . . . and give them good advantage, against a daring adversary [*i.e.* the Spanish] . . .' (Howes *Chronicles*, 1615, pp. 807–8). Drake then searched for a return route through the Strait of Anian and the north-west passage around the extreme north of America. Finding open sea northward but no sign of a passage eastward, he turned south and anchored in a harbour on the coast of California in about 38°N, naming the country 'Nova Albion', and taking possession in the name of Queen Elizabeth I. Obliged to return to England by way of the Pacific and the East Indies, Drake took the opportunity of coming to some sort of trading agreement with the Sultan of Ternate who controlled the clove trade of the Moluccas. His route through the East Indies lay along the uncharted south coast of Java. He found that Java was an island, and not connected to the southern continent as the Dutch apparently believed as late as Cornelis Houtman's voyage of 1596–7. On the south coast Drake anchored probably in the port of Tjilatjap. He went on to complete the second circumnavigation of the world – the next after Magellan's, 1519–22.

Through this voyage he attained as a navigator a rank second only to that of Columbus, Vasco da Gama and Magellan. After his return in 1580 he was knighted at Deptford aboard his ship the *Golden Hind* and settled briefly to a respectable country life at Buckland Abbey. He had risen a long way from his obscure beginnings as a mate on an English coasting vessel.

Called 'El Draque' by the Spaniards, Drake undertook further exploits in the West Indies' raid of 1585–6, and his 'singeing of the King of Spain's beard' at Cadiz in 1587 identified him in popular mythology as the vanquisher of the Spanish Armada in 1588. Despite his popularity he had his critics. His execution of Thomas Doughty at Port St Julian on 2 July 1578 and his high-handed action against William Borough after Cadiz in 1587 both resulted in long drawn-out legal cases. On his last voyage, to the West Indies, 1595–6, he and John Hawkins were given independent commands within the same fleet, an arrangement which may well have contributed to the expedition's failure. Although Drake died on this disastrous voyage, his patriotic reputation was undiminished. As the anonymous author of a unique contemporary broadside records: 'Happy thus the death of Francis Drake, in that whilst due to nature, it was yet for his Country that in chief it was rendered' (**149**).

Mounted in celebration of the quatercentenary of Drake's circumnavigation, 1577–80, the exhibition on display in the King's Library illustrates the career of Sir Francis Drake and in particular his achievements on the 'Famous Voyage', as it became popularly known. The British Library Reference Division inherits from the British Museum Library a rich collection of contemporary accounts and maps, manuscript and printed. These have been supplemented by loans from the British Museum, from other public institutions and from private collections. In addition to various important manuscripts and maps, these loans include coins and medals, American Indian artefacts and weapons, English costume and armour, navigational instruments, an early ship model, and a chair made from the timbers of the *Golden Hind*.

Maps, views and sketches

A number of maps, both manuscript and printed, are associated with the voyage of circumnavigation and with Drake's maritime career. To illustrate the world as Drake knew it, manuscript maps made by the sixteenth century Portuguese chartmakers Diogo Homem and Fernão Vaz Dourado are displayed. Homem's atlas of charts which he made probably in London for presentation to Queen Mary in 1558 illustrates the extent of geographical knowledge of the Far East (**15**), while Vaz Dourado's charts made in Lisbon about 1575 show the Atlantic and South America (**13**). A series of unique watercolour plans of the Spanish fort at San Juan de Ulúa (Vera Cruz) by Cristóbal de Eraso have been generously lent by Hans P. Kraus of New York (**27a, b**). These show the fortifications as they existed about 1570, just two years after Drake's and John Hawkins's treacherous defeat by the Spaniards. Drake's home port of Plymouth is depicted on two manuscript maps in the exhibition; one dated about 1536 shows the harbour and its estuary and is one of the earliest surviving charts of the south coast (**25**); the second describes the watercourse which Drake built from the river Meavy to Plymouth about 1589–90 (**138**). Buckland Abbey is also shown (**109**).

On the voyage of circumnavigation Drake is known to have painted and sketched his own maps and views. Although these do not survive, copies of those drawn by his chaplain, Francis Fletcher, are preserved in a late-seventeenth century transcript of his journal, now Sloane MS 61. The journal illustrates in its maps and text the discovery, *inter alia*, that Tierra del Fuego was an island. One map depicts Elizabeth Island, the southernmost of Drake's discoveries (**58**). For the Strait itself a number of maps illustrate the significance of the popular saying that Drake 'shot the gulf', for the Strait was then the only known western passage to Asia. The length and hazards of the navigation are clearly indicated in Sir John Narborough's large manuscript chart of 1670 – the first detailed survey of the Strait (**51**). This chart is also important for its depiction of the Patagonians and Tierra del Fuegans. Narborough's drawings may be compared with Fletcher's sketches of the artefacts of the Patagonians ('the Giants') and the Tierra del Fuegans, which must rank as the earliest depictions of these particular objects. Ethnographical specimens are also displayed (**60**). Thus Fletcher's sketch of the 'Giants musicall instrument' is illustrated by a Patagonian raw-hide rattle.

Drake's northward route along the Pacific coast of America was recorded on a number of commemorative maps, most of them published some years after his return in 1580. Of particular note is the unique example of a map on a silver medal signed by Michael Mercator (*ca* 1567–1614), the grandson of the celebrated Dutch geographer Gerard Mercator. Made in London in 1589, the silver medal is the earliest extant dated map of Drake's voyage. In 1592 a pair of globes 62 cm in diameter, designed by Emery Molyneux of Lambeth, and engraved by the Dutchman Jodocus Hondius, were published in London, and became famous as the earliest English globes. The terrestrial displays the tracks of the circumnavigations of Drake and of Thomas Cavendish (1586–8). Only one example of the terrestrial globe of 1592 survives (at Petworth House). The magnificent pair belonging to the Honourable Society of the Middle Temple, of which the terrestrial was revised by Hondius to 1603, have been most generously lent and feature as a centre-piece to the exhibition (**76**). Described by their original owner, William Crashaw, preacher at the Middle Temple from 1605 to 1613, as 'one of the fairest paire of globes in Englande', they provide an outstanding record of Elizabethan maritime achievement. Two maps which were published to celebrate the voyages of Drake and Cavendish are the 'Drake broadside map' by Jodocus Hondius, published probably in Amsterdam about 1595 (**78**), and the Dutch and French text editions of the world map engraved by an otherwise unrecorded craftsman Nicola Van Sype about 1583 or later (**88**). Both maps display inset views of places which Drake visited. These include the only contemporary graphic records of 'Portus Novæ Albionis' and of the port on the south coast of Java where Drake anchored.

Illustrating Drake's West Indies Raid of 1585–6 are the series of large engraved battle plans drawn probably by the Italian map-maker, Baptista Boazio, then resident in London. These were first published in the Latin edition of Drake's voyage, *Expeditio Francisci Draki . . . 1588*. An example of this Latin edition with the maps was bequeathed by the bibliophile, Thomas Grenville, with his library to the Trustees of the British Museum in 1846 (**115**), and seems hitherto to have escaped the notice of bibliographers.

For the Armada campaign one of the most important manuscript maps shown is that drawn by the Surveyor of the Queen's Works, Robert Adams, showing Queen Elizabeth going to Tilbury in 1588 to encourage the English troops encamped there (**134.ii**). On the last voyage of

1595–6 Drake took with him a person to sketch and record the coastal profiles and approaches to harbours and anchorages. The resulting manuscript navigational journal is unique and the only English example of such a work to date from the Elizabethan period. The manuscript has been generously lent to the exhibition by the Bibliothèque Nationale (**147**).

Manuscript and printed sources

In December 1577 when Drake set sail, John Dee had completed his learned survey of exploration and discovery, his *General and Rare Memorials*, of which the first volume (1577) provided a prospectus for England's overseas expansion. Entitled *The Pety Navy Royall*, it argued the need for a navy to establish and protect the 'Brytish Impire' thus envisaged. Only this first volume was published (**5**). Dee's manuscript for the fourth and last volume, 'Of Famous and Rich Discoveries', heralded as a 'General Suruey Hydrographicall, of all the whole world', survives in the collections of Sir Robert Cotton (1571–1631), *Cotton MS Vitellius C.VII* (**6**). So secret were the objectives of Drake's voyage to the Pacific that only one set of proposals seems to have survived in manuscript. This is a manuscript memorandum of notes on the voyage, presumably set down for Sir Francis Walsingham to present in 1577 the case for Drake's voyage to the Queen (**37**). Also preserved in the Cotton manuscripts, *Cotton MS Otho E.VIII*, it was partly burnt in 1731 in the Cotton Library fire. Another notable manuscript is a contemporary Portuguese rutter for the Brazilian coast and Strait of Magellan, *ca* 1577, which was apparently translated into English by a Portuguese, and illustrates the detailed navigational knowledge which may well have been available to Francis Drake on his outward voyage (**44**).

Various manuscript accounts of the voyage survive, of which that by Francis Fletcher, *Sloane MS 61* (**58**), is the most comprehensive, but only the first part survives, covering the voyage to the end of November 1578, and concluding with Drake's visit to the island of Mocha off the coast of Chile. The text comprises a later copy made by the physician John Conyers in about 1677. The drawings in the original have been carefully copied, either as an exact copy, or with alterations of size carefully noted (**41,43,58**). Another important narrative is that by a certain John Cooke who sailed on the voyage (**46, 48**). Preserved in the Harley manuscripts (*Harley MS 540, ff. 93ʳ–110ᵛ*), it is written in the hand of the chronicler and antiquary John Stow (1525?–1605), with the heading 'Ser Francis Drake. Anno dñi 1577'. This account throws light on various important aspects of the voyage, including the growing dissension between Drake and Thomas Doughty which led eventually to Doughty's beheading at Port St Julian. Other documents collected by Stow in the Harley manuscripts may include 'Sr Fraunsis Drake's voyage wᵗʰ his proseeding againste Thomas Doughtye', *Harley MS 6221, f.7* (**45**), and the so-called 'Anonymous Narrative', *A discourse of Sir Francis Drakes iorney and exploytes after hee had passed yᵉ Straytes of Megellan into Mare de Sur & through the rest of his voyadge afterward till he arrived in England. 1580. anno, Harley MS 280, ff. 83–90* (**68**). This complements Fletcher's journal as it begins where Fletcher's first part ends. It provides an independent account of Drake's arrival in 'Nova Albion' and his act of possession in the Queen's name. To supplement these narratives the Public Record Office has lent a number of state papers relevant to the voyage. A comprehensive account of Drake's depredations of Spanish ships and towns on the Pacific coast of America is given by the Spaniard San Juan de Anton, master and owner of the *Cacafuego*, whose report was translated into English, presumably to be used as a basis for the charges against Drake on his return (**65**). Another important piece of evidence is the will of Thomas Doughty, together with a codicil probably written on the voyage itself (**47**). This document was brought to light by Peter Penfold and is also lent by the Public Record Office.

On the return of the *Golden Hind* in 1580 the poet Nicholas Breton published a brief laudatory 'Discourse' on Drake's 'happy adventures', known only in one example, now in the collection of Mr Kraus, and kindly lent for the exhibition (**94**). As Breton gives few details of the voyage (and had no authority to do so), the first printed account of the voyage was a treatise by Charles de l'Écluse the celebrated botanist, published in 1582, and comprising notes on the aromatic plants collected by Drake, with details of the circumstances of their discovery (**55**). To commemorate Drake's death in 1596 a broadside memorial in Latin verse was issued. A unique copy from the collection of the Society of Antiquaries is displayed (**149**).

Portraits and memorabilia

Of the contemporary artefacts, coins and medals and portraits generously lent to the exhibition, many come from departments of the British Museum. The Museum of Mankind (the Department of Ethnography of the British Museum) has lent the articles of clothing and artefacts of the Patagonians and Tierra del Fuegans (**60**), the three decorated *keros* or drinking vessels dating from the colonial period of Peru (**22**), and Indian artefacts from the north-west coast of North America (**72**). Among the coins and medals borrowed is an example of the Armada medal (**136**), together with some contemporary Spanish coinage, including a 'piece of eight' (**21**). The Ashmolean Museum has lent a model of an armed trading vessel probably dating from the early Jacobean period (**54**). From the National Maritime Museum comes the navigational compendium made by Humfray Cole and dated 1569, commonly known as 'Drake's dial' (**35**).

The miniatures of Queen Elizabeth I and of Francis Drake painted by Nicholas Hilliard, kindly lent by the Victoria and Albert Museum and the National Portrait Gallery respectively, are displayed side by side (**108, 107**). Navigational instruments include a mariner's astrolabe from the Museum of the History of Science at Oxford (**34**), and from Harriet Wynter Ltd, a lodestone and a replica of a cross-staff (**34a, b**), representing the seaman's navigational aids in the late sixteenth century. A number of pieces of furniture were reputedly made from the timbers of the *Golden Hind* when she was finally broken up, one of which, the chair, is kindly lent to the exhibition by the Bodleian Library (**111**). Last but not least, William Shakespeare in the form of the marble statue by L. F. Roubiliac, signed and dated 1758, casts a discerning eye over Drake and his proceedings. A well-known feature of the King's Library, the statue was formerly in the Temple of Shakespeare in the garden of David Garrick's villa at Hampton, and was bequeathed by Garrick to the British Museum in 1779. Shakespeare's participation is appropriate, for his plays make allusion to the Molyneux globes (**76**), and to the world map of Edward Wright (**79**). In *The Tempest*, Caliban (an anagram of 'cannibal') invokes the deity

Setebos. Referring to the Indians at Port Desire, and following Eden's text of Magellan's voyage, Fletcher writes: 'Yet would they have non of our company, till such tyme they were warranted by oracle from their god Settaboth, that is, the Divell, whom they name their great god'. Finally, when Rosalind declares in *As you like it* (III.ii), 'one inch of delay more is a South-sea of Discovery', she conjures up the wonders of the Pacific which Drake first revealed to his fellow-countrymen.

Helen Wallis
Map Librarian

Acknowledgements

The exhibition has been organized jointly by the Map Library of the Department of Printed Books and the Department of Manuscripts. Its preparation was the work of Sarah Tyacke, Helen Wallis, and Pat Higgins, who also are responsible for the catalogue, the text of which was edited by Sarah Tyacke and checked by Gillian Barrett. The design of the exhibition has been undertaken by Bob Aitken of the Design Office of the British Museum. The maps prepared for the catalogue were drawn by John Mitchell.

The organizers also wish to express their thanks to all those who helped in the preparation of the exhibition and the catalogue. Peter Penfold and Hilary Jones of the Public Record Office have been unsparing in their efforts in searching the records and making the necessary arrangements for the loan of seventeen items. Elizabeth Carmichael and Jonathan King of the Museum of Mankind have given valuable help in selecting the ethnographical specimens for display. Brian Smith, County Archivist of Gloucestershire, gave useful information on John Wynter and drew attention to the declaration of acquittal from charges of piracy drawn up in 1582 for Wynter (98). Alwyn Wheeler and Phyllis Edwards of the British Museum (Natural History) helped in the identification of the botanical specimens and fish which Drake and his company observed or collected on the circumnavigation, and W. T. Stearn gave information on *Winteranus Cortex* (55). Thanks are also due to Felix Hull, County Archivist of Kent, for his help with the records relating to Drake's family and early career; to Rodney Dennys, Somerset Herald, College of Arms, for advice and information about Drake's arms; to Robert Chell of the Devon Record Office who supplied information about Drake's first marriage and a copy of the entry in the St Budeaux parish register. Raymond Aker of the Drake Navigators Guild kindly offered a number of photographs of the north-west coast of America and also the drawings of his reconstruction of the *Golden Hind*'s track. Brigadier E. L. H. Smith, Custodian of Berkeley Castle, has lent a photograph of the camphor wood chest reputed to have belonged to Drake. Robert Latham, Librarian of the Pepys Library, Magdalene College, Cambridge, arranged for photographs to be made of 'Drake's tide-tables', the *Libro de cargos*, and the picture of the *Jesus of Lübeck*. Paul Mellon of Upperville provided a photograph of his manuscript map showing Drake's circumnavigation and his West Indies' Raid, 1585–6 (75). Members of the staff of the National Maritime Museum have given much help and advice, notably Derek Howse of the Department of Astronomy, Alan Stimson of the Department of Navigation, and John Munday of the Department of Armour and Weapons. Additional nautical and historical material was provided by G. P. B. Naish, Secretary of the Society for Nautical Research.

Within the British Library Reference Division the organizers would like to thank, for all their help in setting up the exhibition, D. H. Turner, Janet Backhouse, Mirjam Foot, Ernest Jones, Yolande O'Donoghue, Shelley Jones, Mike Chambers, and Vic Carter.

I

English voyages before Drake

'IN this most famous and peerleese governement of her most excellent Majesty, her subjects . . . in searching the most opposite corners and quarters of the world . . . in compassing the vaste globe of the earth more then once, have excelled all the nations and people of the earth.' Richard Hakluyt addressed these stirring words to Sir Francis Walsingham in the Epistle Dedicatorie to *The Principall Navigations . . . of the English nation . . .* (1589). No one regretted more than he to hear the English condemned for their 'sluggish security' and past neglect of overseas discovery and enterprise. When Queen Elizabeth's subjects cast ambitious eyes beyond the narrow seas of Europe in the early years of her reign, they found the richest lands and commerce already annexed by Spain and Portugal. Hakluyt might well contest on paper (as in his *Discourse of Western Planting*, 1584) this arrogant division of the world into two spheres, western and eastern, commanded by Spain and Portugal (to be united in 1580 in a single empire). Privateers like Drake and Hawkins likewise pursued their own private or semi-official wars, seeking trade and fortune in forbidden territories by force of arms. Nevertheless, an outright challenge to the Hispanic powers awaited a later generation, when England had established herself among the major powers of Europe.

Finding their field of enterprise circumscribed, Englishmen turned their attention in the 1550s and 1560s to new routes and unoccupied lands. The chief goal of exploration was the wealth of the Orient, notably of Cathay and the Spice Islands (the Moluccas), 'the most richest londes and ilondes in the worlde, for all the gold, spices, aromatikes and pretiose stones . . . from thens thei come', Roger Barlow, an English merchant in Seville, wrote to King Henry VIII in 1541. The route to the East by way of the Cape of Good Hope was the monopoly of Portugal. It seemed therefore that the northern passages to Asia were especially reserved for England's discovery and exploitation, in view of her late start and her north-westerly position in Europe. Barlow's friend Robert Thorne, another merchant trading in Seville, wrote in his address to King Henry VIII, *ca* 1531 (**1**): 'There is one way to discouer, which is unto the North, for out of Spaine they have discovered all the Indies and Seas Occidentall, and out of Portugal all the Indies and Seas Orientall.' The 'forme of a Mappe' which he sent from Seville, illustrating this polar route, was engraved and published in Hakluyt's *Divers Voyages* (1582) (**2, 10**). By the middle of the sixteenth century the lands encircling the North Pole on contemporary maps discouraged the idea of a polar passage. Debate now turned on the relative merits of the north-west and the north-east passages. The geographical consultant and mathematician Dr John Dee and the geographical editor Richard Eden favoured the north-east passage. Eden's friend Richard Chancellor sailed with Sir Hugh Willoughby on the first English expedition to the north-east in 1553, on which Chancellor reached Moscow. A second expedition under Chancellor in 1555 established trade with Russia for pursuance of which the Muscovy Company was founded in the same year. On the third expedition of 1556–7, Stephen Borough and his sixteen-year-old brother William (in his later years Clerk of the Queen's ships and Drake's vice-admiral on the Cadiz expedition 1587) reached the Kara Sea. Borough and Dee drew up the instructions for Pet and Jackman's disastrous voyage of 1580, whose failure was to be mitigated by Drake's triumphant return.

Interest meanwhile had turned in the 1560s and 1570s to the north-west passage. The colonial entrepreneur Sir Humphrey Gilbert in his treatise *A Discourse of a Discovery for a new passage to Cataia*, written in 1566, argued that the north-west passage 'were the onely way for our princes, to possesse ye welth of all the East partes . . . of the Worlde', on account of the shortness of the voyage, and the fact that it was outside the jurisdictions of Spain and Portugal. Published in 1576, the *Discourse* (**4**) served as propaganda for Martin Frobisher's first voyage in search of the north-west passage, 1576. On this voyage Frobisher discovered 'Frobisher's Straits', which were in reality a bay on the west coast of Baffin Island. In May 1577, seven months before Drake sailed for the South Seas, Frobisher set out on his second voyage, bringing home 200 tons of supposed gold ore. A fleet of fifteen ships was mustered for the third voyage, 1578, on which Frobisher sailed 60 leagues into Hudson's Strait, called 'the Mistaken Straits', and believed to lead to the Pacific (**6–9**). Drake had with him in the *Golden Hind* a map which marked the north-west passage in 66°N, as the Portuguese pilot Nuño da Silva was to report. This must have been Gilbert's map in the *Discourse* (**4**) or the large world map of Ortelius, 1564 (**61**), from which Gilbert's was derived. Aided by one or other, Drake was seeking the western end of the passage eleven months after Frobisher had discovered what he supposed was its eastern entrance.

Associated with the search for the north-west passage were the projects for English colonization of North America, of which Sir Humphrey Gilbert and Richard Hakluyt were leading advocates. The discoveries of John Cabot and his son Sebastian on their voyages of 1497 and 1498 (their individual achievements were confused in sixteenth century records) gave England her title to the occupation and settlement of the northern parts of North America. Such plantations would be profitable in their own right, and also would aid the search for the north-west passage, as Hakluyt argued in his *Divers Voyages touching the discouerie of America* (1582) (**10**), the first English handbook for the colonization of North America.

That such projects demanded the development of English sea power and improvement in navigational practices was John Dee's thesis in his remarkable tetralogy, *General and Rare Memorials pertayning to the Perfect Art of Navigation*. In the first volume, published in 1577, Dee proposed the creation of a 'Pety-Navy-Royall' and he prophesied Britain's imperial destiny, arguing 'the lawfull and very honorable Entitling of our . . . Queene Elizabeth . . . to very large Forrein Dominions' (**5**). The other surviving volume, preserved in manuscript, comprised a geographical treatise on English and foreign discoveries, and recommended for England the discovery of the north-east passage, although Dee commended Frobisher's exploits then in hand (**6**).

Successful colonial and commercial expansion overseas demanded knowledge of past discoveries, especially those of Spain and Portugal. Richard Eden led the way in translating and publishing in 1555 Peter Martyr's *Decades of the New World* (**3**), which Richard Willes expanded in his edition in 1577 (**31c**). In the next generation this was to be Hakluyt's self-appointed role, as editor, translator, and sponsor of the publication of many foreign works as well as of his own three great collections of '*Voyages*'. The chronicle of how Spain and Portugal had achieved their mighty empires was a matter of urgent interest as England entered the field.

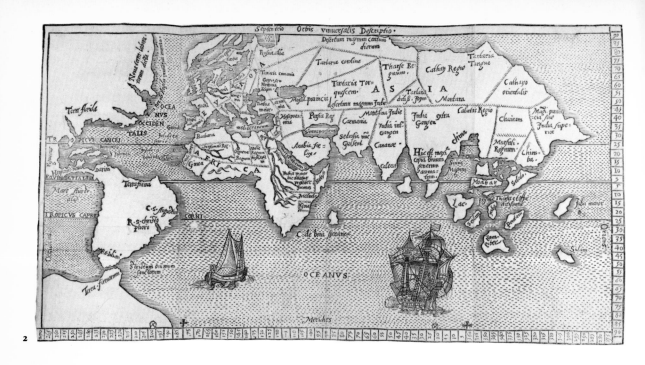

2

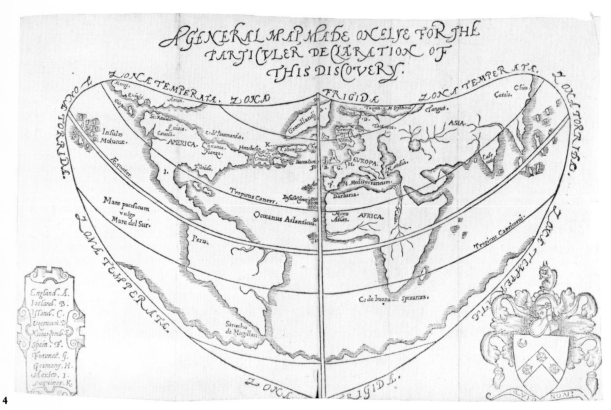

4

18

1   A northern route to China

Address of Robert Thorne to King Henry VIII.
MS 31 cm   *Cotton MS Vitellius C.VII. f.342*^r

Composed about 1531 to accompany a copy of a letter which Thorne, a Bristol merchant resident in Seville, had written in 1527 to Dr Edward Lee (afterwards Archbishop of York), then engaged on an embassy to Spain. This letter, which dealt with the possibility of a route to Cathay through northern waters, produced no immediate result, but it exercised a profound influence on English exploration during the next fifty years and may be said to have initiated the search for the north-west passage. Thorne's dictum 'No sea innavigable, no land unhabitable' was to become a guiding principle of English overseas enterprise.

The present manuscript is a copy made, about 1577, for Dr John Dee, to whom the original documents had been sent by Cyprian Lucar, whose father Emanuel Lucar, a prominent London merchant, had been executor to Thorne. The documents were repeatedly printed by Hakluyt.

2   Robert Thorne's world map, 1527

Septentrio Orbis Universalis Descriptio.
In: Richard Hakluyt *Divers Voyages*. London, 1582.
23 × 44 cm   C.21.b.35

'This is the forme of a Mappe sent 1527. from Siuill in Spayne by maister Robert Thorne marchaunt, to Doctor Ley Embassadour for king Henry the 8. to Charles the Emperour', Richard Hakluyt explains in his caption, excusing the 'rudeness' of the map. Although at the time of publication (1582) it was fifty years out of date, it had a historic interest as a picture of the world not long after Magellan's voyage (1519–22). If it represents the original map drawn by Thorne in 1527 (or earlier), the work ranks as the earliest surviving post-mediæval world map to have been drawn by an Englishman.

3   Discovery of the New World

Richard Eden. *The Decades of the newe worlde or west India . . . Written in the Latine tounge by Peter Martyr of Angleria, and translated into Englysshe by Rycharde Eden.* London, W. Powell, 1555.
18 cm   C.13.a.8

Richard Eden's *Decades* is the earliest travel collection in English, and his second work of translation. It contains not only his version of Peter Martyr's first three *Decades*, describing the discovery of America, but also translations from the Spanish chronicles of Oviedo and Gomara and from other narratives of the Spanish and Portuguese discoveries. These include various accounts of Magellan's voyage round the world (ff. 214–235), which were consulted and read aloud on Drake's voyage (see **31**). Of special interest for Englishmen was the report of the discovery of the north-west passage by Sebastian Cabot, made in his youth while in the service of England (ff. 118^v–19^r), and the narratives of English voyages to Guinea, 1553–4 (ff. 343–360).

Although the book showed English readers only too clearly how much had been achieved by Spain in the conquest of the New World, its preface included some words of encouragement for future English enterprise: 'besyde the portion of lande perteyning to the Spanyardes (being eyght tymes bygger then Italye . . .) . . . there yet remayneth an other portion of that mayne lande reachyinge towarde the north-east, thought to be as large as the other, and not yet knowen but only by the sea coastes, neyther inhabyted by any Christian men . . . in this lande there are many fayre and frutefull regions . . . (sig.C.1^r).

4   The north-west passage to China

Sir Humphrey Gilbert. A General Map, made onelye for the particular declaration of this discovery. In: *A Discovrse of a Discouerie for a New Passage to Cataia*, London, 1576.
19 cm   C.32.b.29

Sir Humphrey Gilbert, a leading advocate of the search for a north-west passage to China (Cataia) and the Far East, wrote in 1566 his treatise on the likelihood and advantages of its discovery. Having consulted 'Mappes and Globes both Antique & Moderne', he sets out many arguments to prove from the insularity of America the existence of the passage. He shows the route by the north-west to be a discovery more probable and profitable than that by the north-east, which hitherto had been favoured by explorers, merchants and geographers such as John Dee. The wood-cut map included in the published work illustrates these arguments. Drawn on a cordiform projection, it is a much reduced version of Ortelius's large world map of 1564 (**61**). America is depicted as an island with an open passage to the North, whereas the north-east passage (as on Ortelius's map) is cut off on account of the continuation of Asia to the top right-hand edge of the border.

The publication of the *Discourse* in 1576 (ostensibly without Gilbert's permission) was an advertisement for Frobisher's Company of Cathay which despatched in that year the first expedition to the north-west in search of the Passage. It is probable that Drake had with him a copy of Dee's *Discourse* with the map.

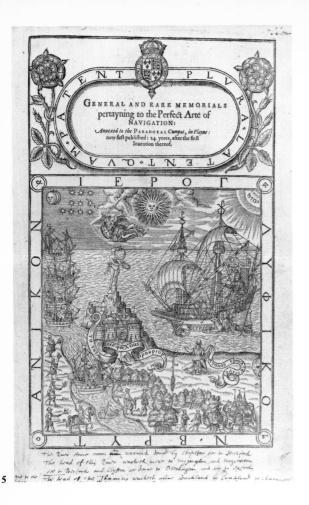

5

5 England's imperial destiny

John Dee. *General and Rare Memorials pertayning to the Perfect Arte of Navigation.* London, John Daye, 1577.
MS additions 33 cm   C.21.e.12

John Dee wrote his *General and Rare Memorials* as the first volume of a work on the 'British Empire', in which, like Hakluyt, he predicted the imperial and maritime destiny of England. The first volume sets out the argument for establishing a 'Pety Navy Royall, continually to be mainteyned, for manifold great Commodities procuring to this Brytish Monarchie' (sig.E.iii^v). The Navy should number 'Threescore Tall Ships, and eche of them, betwene eightscore and two hundred, Tun of Burden: And Twenty other smaller Barks'. The hieroglyphic frontispiece shows Queen Elizabeth at the helm of the Christian ship of Europe, a forecast of England as mistress of the seas. The title seems to be intended as the general title of the whole work, of which this was the only volume printed (in 100 copies). The volume is dedicated to Sir Christopher Hatton, Captain of the Queen's bodyguard and gentleman of her privy chamber (who also was Drake's patron).

This copy is inscribed 'Captain Hichcoks Book the gift of Dockter Dee [15]77'. Captain Thomas Hickock, a member of the Barbary Company, was responsible for the English translations of the travels of Cesare dei Fedrici (Caesar Frederick) in Asia, published in London in 1588, and reprinted by Hakluyt in the *Principal Navigations* (1598–1600).

6 Famous and rich discoveries

John Dee. The Great Volume of Famous and Riche Discoveries.
MS 31 cm   *Cotton MS Vitellius C.vii, ff. 178^b, 179*

This work, written in the spring and early summer of 1577, was the last volume of Dee's great geographical tetralogy, *General and Rare Memorials pertayning to the Perfect Art of Navigation*. Only the first volume, *The Pety Navy Royall (5)*, was printed. The second volume, entitled *Queen Elizabeth her Tables Gubernautik*, is lost, and the third was intentionally destroyed; the fourth survives in the present manuscript which is in Dee's autograph throughout.

The main part of the work consists of a sustained argument for the north-east passage to Cathay, and includes an allusion to Frobisher's second expedition in search of the north-west passage, setting out on 26 May 1577: 'of how great Importance then i[magine] you is that Attempt which is by a Brytish [sub]iect presently intended to God's Glory, the benef[it of] all Christendome & the honor & profit of this R[ealme] chiefly, & contentment of many a Noble mynde t[hat] delighteth to understand, how, Domini est Terra [et] Plenitudo eius, Orbis Terrarum et Universi qui habit[ant] in eo. Who (God sparing life & health) hath res[olute]ly offred up to God and to his Naturall Soverayn & Country the employing of all his skill [and] talent, & the patient enduring of the great toyle of his body to that plac being the very end of the world from us to be reckoned to accomplish that Discovery wch of so many & so valiant captayns by land & by sea hath byn so oft attempted in vayn.' The misreading of 'res[olute]ly' as 'se[cret]ly' led E. G. R. Taylor to construe this passage as a reference to Drake's intended South Sea voyage.

7 Frobisher's voyages

George Best. *A Trve Discovrse of the late voyages of discouerie, for the finding of a passage to Cathaya, by the Northvvest, vnder the conduct of Martin Frobisher Generall.* London, Henry Bynnyman, 1578.
18 cm   G.6527

Frobisher's three Arctic voyages of 1576, 1577 and 1578 were the first of the Elizabethan expeditions in search of the north-west passage. On Frobisher's return in 1578 a copy of this narrative by Best, one of Frobisher's officers, came into the hands of the printer who issued it without consulting the author. It is dedicated to Sir Christopher Hatton (Drake's patron).
   The woodcut map illustrating the discoveries shows Frobisher's Strait (really an inlet on the west coast of Davis Strait) as a northern passage dividing polar lands from America. The map is believed to have been drawn by James Beare, the principal surveyor of the Frobisher expeditions.

8 Map of the north-west passage 1578

Map to illustrate Frobisher's voyages in search of a north-west passage, 1576–8.
In: George Best *A Trve Discovrse of the late voyages of discouerie.* London, 1578.
30 × 39 cm   Maps 978.(44.)

Frobisher's Strait discovered on the voyage of 1576 is here erroneously shown to the south of Greenland and to the north of America. 'The Mistaken Straightes' are the entrance to Hudson's Strait, which Frobisher accidentally discovered on his third voyage while looking for his own strait. With its inscription 'The way trendin to Cathaia', the map thus encouraged the idea of a navigable north-west passage to Asia. Like the general map published with Best's text (7) this woodcut map is probably by James Beare.

9 Eskimos seen on Frobisher's second voyage

Pictura vel delineatio hominum nuper ex Anglia advectorum . . . .
In: [D. Settle] *De Martini Forbisseri Angli navigatione in regiones occidentis et septentriouis Narratio historica . . . Transalata per D. Joan. Tho. Freigum.* Noribergae, 1580.
13 × 17 cm   790.b.1.(1)

In this woodcut engraving, probably derived from a drawing by the English artist John White, eskimos are depicted hunting seabirds. On shore there is a summer encampment of sealskin tents. The book comprises a version (published in Latin, and also in German) of Dionyse Settle's report of Frobisher's second voyage.

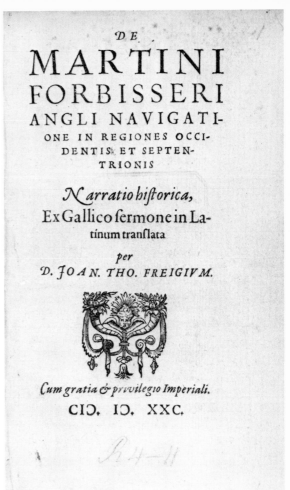

DE
MARTINI FORBISSERI
ANGLI NAVIGATI-
ONE IN REGIONES OCCI-
DENTIS ET SEPTEN-
TRIONIS

Narratio historica,
Ex Gallico sermone in La-
tinum translata

per
D. JOAN. THO. FREIGIVM.

Cum gratia & privilegio Imperiali.
CIƆ. IƆ. XXC.

9i

9ii

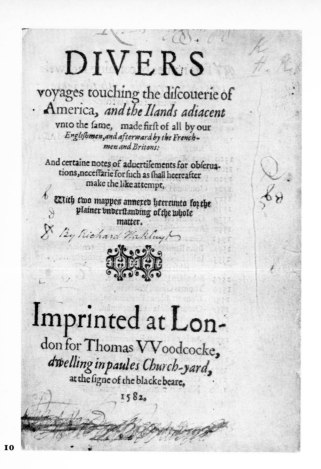

10

Divers voyages touching the discouerie of America . . . . [By Richard Hakluyt.] London, Thomas Woodcocke, 1582.
18 cm   *C.21.b.35*

Richard Hakluyt compiled and published his *Divers voyages* as an encouragement to English enterprise in furthering the discovery, exploration and settlement of North America. In the 'Epistle Dedicatorie', addressed to Sir Philip Sydney and signed R.H., he expounds his argument that as a matter of right through priority of discovery and to 'aduaunce the honour of our Countrie', England should take possession of these lands. Colonies would relieve the country of its 'superfluous people' and would advance the discovery of passages to Asia round or through America. The book is also notable as the earliest geographical text to refer to Drake's voyage. 'Francis Drake Englishman' is entered under 1578 in the list of 'names of certaine late trauaylers'; his discoveries 'on the back side of America' are noted as encouraging the hope of finding a north-west passage, and are recorded on the accompanying map (11). Hakluyt reveals that he has been discussing with Drake his project of establishing in London a lecture in the art of navigation, and has secured from him a promise of financial help.

In this copy, from the library of George Chalmers, the name Richard Hakluyt added in MS at the end of the 'Epistle Dedicatorie' may be Hakluyt's autograph signature.

11   **Lok's map of North America**

Illustri viro, domino Philippo Sidnæo Michael Lok civis Londinensis hanc chartam dedicabat: 1582.
In: Richard Hakluyt *Divers voyages.* London, 1582.
39 × 28 cm   *C.21.b.35*

For the *Divers Voyages* Hakluyt obtained a woodcut map of northern regions from Michael Lok, a leading advocate of the north-west passage to Asia and promoter of Frobisher's expeditions in 1576–8. Lok's map, which showed both a sea route (through Frobisher's Strait) and an easy land passage (across an isthmus in 40 N.) between the Atlantic and the Pacific, supported Hakluyt's argument that a colony in America would advance English trade with the Far East. The reference off the coast of 'Sierra Nevada' in California to the navigations of the English ('Anglorum [navigationes] 1580') provides the first record of Drake's voyage on a printed map.

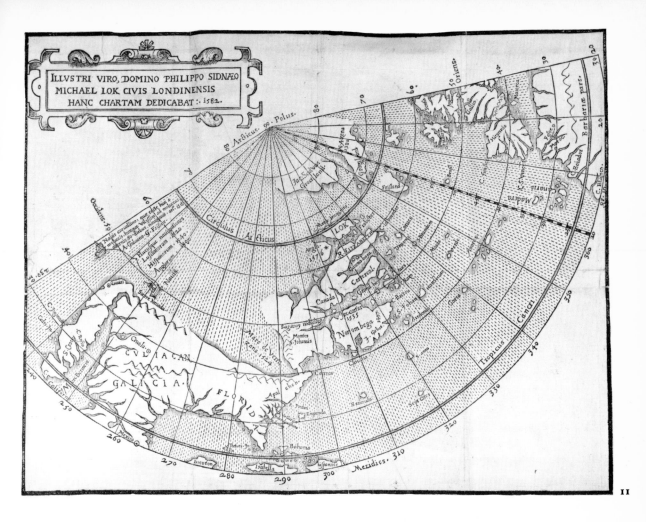

II

The Spanish and Portuguese empires

IN 1492 Christopher Columbus, under the patronage of Spain, set sail for the East Indies across the Atlantic and found the West Indies. Less than thirty years later the rich New World of America was conquered and settled, by the Spanish in New Spain and by the Portuguese in Brazil. In 1498 Vasco da Gama, sailing via the Cape of Good Hope, reached India and the spice markets of Calicut and Goa. Thenceforward the 'royal grocers of Europe', as Francis I enviously dubbed the Portuguese Kings, came to control by force the East Indies' trade in pepper, cloves and other spices, at once necessities and luxuries in sixteenth-century Europe. Although dissimilar in character, the colonial empire of Spain and the trading empire of Portugal both fiercely protected their respective monopolies. This exclusive division of the world into Portuguese and Spanish spheres presented an alluring and inevitable challenge to English, French and Dutch interlopers.

By 1575 an estimated 69,000 colonists had settled in the New World. In the words of Bernal Díaz, soldier and chronicler of Cortés' expedition to Mexico, the Spanish went to America 'to serve God and His Majesty, to give light to those in darkness, and also to get rich'. Most of the settlers would have approved of the first two aspirations, but all pursued the last one, even if their wealth derived from ranching or planting sugar cane rather than from mining gold or silver. That the empire was not only rich but also Catholic gave added reason for assault to the Protestant sailors from France, England and the Low Countries, to none more so than Francis Drake. But against the hope of plunder which lay open to enterprising pirates and privateers was set the strength of the empire: the fortified ports of Santo Domingo in Hispaniola, Havana in Cuba, Nombre de Dios, Puerto Bello and Cartagena on the Atlantic mainland. Along the Pacific coast stood Panama and Callao, the port of Lima in Peru. The colonial provinces were governed satisfactorily for the most part, and were subject to the Council of the Indies in Madrid. The convoy system for the treasure fleets which sailed from Havana each year to Spain rarely failed, and the bullion route across the isthmus from Panama to Nombre de Dios was well established. Thus in the 1560s the Spanish empire was strong, and more than a match for the colonizing activities of the French in Florida, where the settlers were summarily executed by Pedro Menéndez in 1565. The Spanish were not able, however, to prevent interlopers and pirates from sailing to the Caribbean in search of trade and bullion. The most inventive and opportunist of these was Francis Drake.

12 The first circumnavigation 1519–22

Carta Uniuersal En que Se contiene todo lo que del mundo se ha descubierto fasto agora. Hizola Diego Ribero cosmographo de Su magestad: Anõ de: 1529, ẽ Sevjlla.
A reduced reproduction by W. Griggs (published in 1886) of the manuscript map formerly in the Library of the Roman Congregation, *De Propaganda Fide*, now in the Vatican Library.
61 × 141 cm (size of original MS 85 × 204 cm)

Maps S.T.W.I

In 1494, in accordance with the provisions of the Treaty of Tordesillas, an imaginary line dividing the Spanish and Portuguese zones of colonial and commercial interest was established 370 leagues west of the Azores; the Spanish to the west, the Portuguese to the east. The Americas, with the exception of Brazil, lay on the Spanish side of the line.

On this official world chart (detail illustrated) drawn by Diogo Ribeiro, a Portuguese by birth but in the employ of the Casa de la Contración in Seville, the line is indicated by the presence of Spanish and Portuguese flags. In the eastern hemisphere the position of the line had not been settled and the disputed area of the Moluccas is clearly shown on the chart by the setting of the national flags some distance apart. In 1529 Charles V of Spain ceded his claim to the islands and the line was laid down 17 degrees east of the Moluccas. The chart also shows the discoveries of Ferdinand Magellan whose voyage round the world was completed in 1522. A number of Spanish ships can be seen plying to and from the East Indies. Off the east coast of South America and in the south Pacific beyond the Strait of Magellan are shown ships with the accompanying legend, *voy a Maluco* (I go to the Moluccas), which are surely intended to represent Magellan's newly found route and his ship the *Vitoria*. Another version is preserved in Thuringische Landesbibliothek, Weimar (detail illustrated from a facsimile).

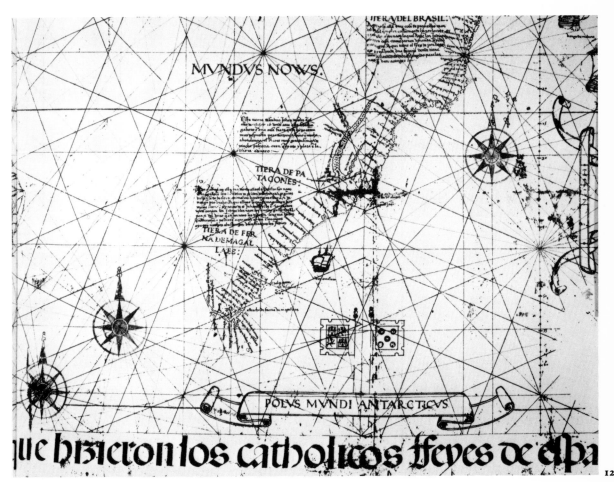

13 Charting the New World

A chart of South America, with a running title in the border: 'Nesta lamina esta lamcado o Boqveirão de Fernao de Magalhais ate o Rio da Prata.'
In a manuscript atlas 'Universalis et integra totius orbis hidrographia ad verrissimam Luzitanorum traditionem descripcio Ferdinado Vã', 1575, f. 3.
MS coloured 39 × 52 cm   *Additional MS 31317*

Fernão Vaz Dourado, the cartographer who drew this atlas of the world and dedicated it to King Sebastian of Portugal (1554–78), is known to have made six such atlases from 1568 to 1580. Born about 1520 in Diu, a small town in Gujerat, then part of the Portuguese trading empire centred on the port of Goa, Vaz Dourado became one of the finest of the Portuguese cartographers who dominated the profession of chart making in the sixteenth century. Although many of his charts were made in Goa, this atlas was probably drawn in Lisbon, as, unlike those he drew in India, the tide-tables (f. 19) are set for use on the western coast of the Iberian peninsula. The same folio bears the date '1575', and the atlas may therefore have been drawn in that year.

The world chart said to have been made for Francis Drake in Lisbon for his voyage round the world has been conjecturally identified as one by Vaz Dourado, and, if this supposition is correct, it may be assumed to be a compilation made from those charts which appear in his atlases.

14 The Portuguese trading empire

Anfa, quibusdam Anaffa [Casablanca]; Azaamurum [Azemmour]; Diu; Goa fortissima Indiae urbs in Christianorum potestatem anno Salutis 1509 devenit.
In: G. Braun and F. Hogenberg *Civitates Orbis Terrarum.* [Cologne, 1573–1618.] Lib. I, no. 57.
42 × 52 cm   *Maps C.7.d.1*

The voyages of Vasco da Gama (1497–8) and of Pedro Alvares Cabral (1500–1) laid the foundations of the Portuguese trading empire in India and the East Indies. King Manoel assumed the title 'Lord of the Conquest, navigation and commerce of Ethiopia, Arabia, Persia and India', and through the *Casa da Mina e India* controlled the spice trade by a series of forts and factories built at strategic points along the shipping

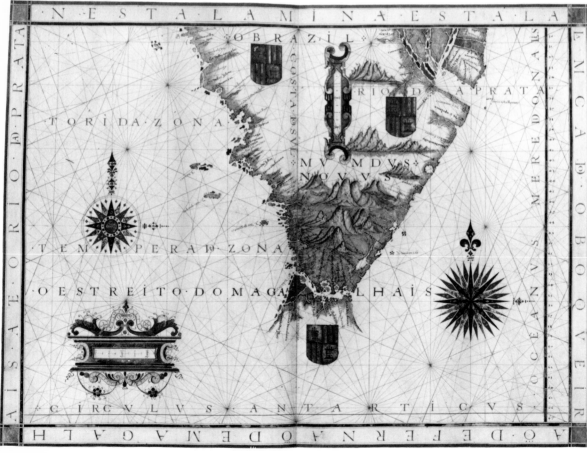

13

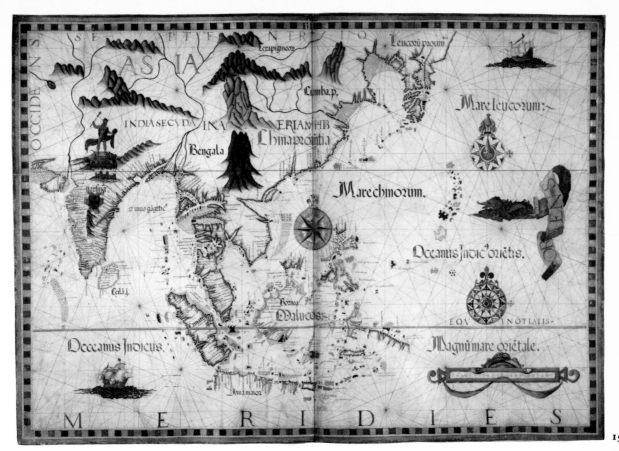

routes. The capital of this empire was Goa, conquered in 1509 by Afonso de Albuquerque. In the East Indies itself the spice trade from the Moluccas, notably from the island of Ternate, was organized by the factory at Malacca on the Malay Peninsula.

The engraved views of Goa and Diu in Gujerat province, included by Georg Braun and Francis Hogenberg in their *Civitates Orbis Terrarum*, were probably based on a Portuguese manuscript illustrated by views. This cannot now be identified, but it must have been similar to the surviving *Lendas da Indias* of Gaspar Correia who sailed with Albuquerque. The manuscript which was completed by 1564 is now in the Torre do Tombo in Lisbon. Also shown are smaller views of the Moroccan ports of Azemmour and Casablanca (Anfa), which was captured by the Portuguese in 1468 and rebuilt in 1515.

15 Charting the Spice Islands

A chart of the coasts of the Far East from India to Japan, including the islands of the East Indies.
In an atlas of twelve manuscript charts drawn by Diogo Homem in 1558, f. 9.
MS coloured 59 × 82 cm   *Additional MS 5415.A*

The son of Lopo Homem (fl. 1517–54), chartmaker in Lisbon, Diogo is known to have made twelve highly decorative atlases of the world and eleven world charts in the period 1547–76. He is first recorded in London in 1547, where he had fled after being accused of the murder of one Antonio Fernandes in Lisbon. In London he was evidently making his living by drawing charts. Giving evidence before the High Court of Admiralty, he affirmed that he had made a world chart on eight sheets which was worth about 100 ducats. Although offered a pardon by the King John III of Portugal in August 1547, Homem seems to have remained an exile and is thought to have made this atlas in London for presentation to Queen Mary.

Homem's involvement in English overseas expeditions does not seem to have been confined to cartography. In September 1567 the Spanish ambassador, Guzman de Silva, wrote to Philip II telling him of the imminent departure of John Hawkins's ships from Plymouth and the intention of various Portuguese to go with them, presumably as pilots and negotiators with the Portuguese in West Africa. He then wrote: 'some ten days ago arrived here [*i.e.* London] another Portuguese, called Diogo Homem, who was to go with them, and they imprisoned him immediately and keep him in such a manner that they do not let him speak to anyone'; a necessary precaution in view of Hawkins's ultimate destination in the Caribbean. Diogo was a close relative (possibly even a brother) of André Homem, the Portuguese cosmographer to the French crown, who had also interested himself in Hawkins's Guinea ventures.

This chart of the East Indies reflects the state of knowledge throughout the middle decades of the sixteenth century and was, through the work of the chartmaker, Bartolemeu Lasso, perpetuated in Jan Huyghen van Linschoten's *Itinerario*, published at Amsterdam in 1595.

16   Philip II of Spain (1527–1598)

Philippus II Caroli V filius Hispaniarum, Indiarū . . . Rex Cathol . . . Aetatis suae 59. Effigiem hanc Sereniss^ae Isabella Clarae Eugeniae dicti Regis Filiae in devoti animi testimonium dedicat consecrata. Joannes Eillarts Frisius Sculptor.
44 × 33 cm *Lent by B.M. Department of Prints and Drawings, 1871-12-9-838*

The character and efficiency of government within the Spanish empire in America were moulded to a large extent by the industrious zeal of King Philip II who 'ruled his empire from his desk', endlessly writing letters to, and annotating dispatches from, the Council of the Indies.

He was born in 1527 and succeeded to the Spanish throne in 1556 on the abdication of his father, Charles V. Not only Spain, but the Low Countries, Naples, Sicily and the Spanish colonial empire were his to rule for the next forty-two years. In 1580 the Portuguese empire was also subjected to his government. According to contemporaries, he was a solitary, secretive person whose high sense of national duty seems to have overidden any natural spontaneity he may have had. He received the news of the Armada's defeat in 1588 with the same equanimity as the triumph of Lepanto in 1571. His caution and prudence, surely necessary for the ruler of so vast an empire, were frequently derided and mistaken for procrastination and indecision. The sorrows of his private life were only relieved by the solace afforded him by his loving daughters Katherine and Isabella. This portrait of Philip in late middle-age by the Dutch engraver Jan Eillarts was dedicated to Isabella, the *Infanta*, in 1586.

17   Governing Spanish America

Descripcion de las Indias Ocidentales de Antonio de Herrera Coronista Mayor desu Mag^d de las Indias y su coronista de Castilla. [By Antonio de Herrera.] Madrid, 1601.
29 cm   *601.k.13*

By the 1570s the Council of the Indies, under the presidency of Juan de Ovando, was a well-informed and efficient governing body. Its nine members formed a standing committee acting as a Supreme Court of Appeal as well as supervising the work of the Colonial *audiencias* or provinces of Spanish America. In 1571 the post of *Cronista Mayor* was established with the purpose of collecting detailed descriptions about the *audiencias*, including statistics about population, and accounts of the provinces' geography and natural products. Antonio de Herrera was appointed *cronista* in 1596, and utilized the collection of reports sent to the council to write his own *Historia General* of the Indies, which was eventually published in eight parts in 1601.

The title page to the 'Description of the West Indies' depicts some of the gods worshiped in New Spain by the Indians, which still remained powerful despite enforced Catholic proselytizing. On the left of the title panel kneels the figure of the god of the dead, and on the right sits the god *Huizilopochtli* to whom an Indian makes an offering. Beneath them are depicted gods described here as gods of wind, water, wine and clowns. At the bottom left the artist has drawn a portrait of the author during his term of office as *cronista*.

18   Seville in the sixteenth century

Sevilla. In: G. Braun and F. Hogenberg *Civitates Orbis Terrarum.* [Cologne, 1573–1617]. Lib. 4, no. 2.
42 × 52 cm   *Maps C.7.d.1*

The centre of Spain's transatlantic trade, Seville was a harbour for small ships set forty miles up the winding Guadalquivir river. With its outport of Sanlúcar it attempted to maintain a monopoly of the American trade, which was fiercely challenged by the more northerly port of Cadiz. By the 1550s, as a result of the constant wars with the French, goods and bullion were carried across the Atlantic in protected convoys. In April or May the *flota* sailed for Vera Cruz in New Spain, in August the *galeones* for Nombre de Dios in Panama, the Atlantic port for trade with Peru. For the return journey to the Guadalquivir river the combined fleets met at Havana. Once in the Caribbean the ships, like Spanish settlements, became the prey of both French and English pirates.

16

17

SEVIL LA

RIO DE GUADALQVEVIR

1 Arraual dela puerta de Carmona	5 Castilleia de Guzman	9 Cerro de Carmona	13 Islesia mator	17 Plaza de Don Pedro Ponze	21 La Madalena	25 Puerta de Triana	29 Puerta de Macarena	33 Puerta de Carmona	37 Torre dela Plata
2 Arraual dela puerta de Macarena	6 Castilleia dela Cuesta	10 El Matadero	14 Monasterio de S.Pablo	18 Plaza de Arcos	22 La Alameda	26 Puerta de Goles	30 Puerta del Sal	34 Puerta de la Corne	38 Torre dellas Huelle
3 Casso del Duq. de Alcala	7 Camas	11 El guemadero	15 Plaza de S.Francisco	19 Plaza de Palacio	23 Monasterio del Carmen	27 Puerta de le Juan	31 Puerta de la Corne	35 Torre de Oro	39 Puerto de Triana
4 Cassa de Colon	8 Calle delas armas	12 El Alcaba	16 Plaza del Duq. de Medina	20 Plaza del Rey	24 Puerta dela Arenal	28 Puer dela almenilla	32 Puerta del Osorio	36 Torre del Oro	40 Las Atarazanas

18

19

19 The Treasure House of the World

Nigritae in scrutandis venis metallicis ab Hispanis
in Insulas ablegantur.
In: T. de Bry, *Americae pars quinta*. Francoforti,
1594. pl. I
35 × 23 cm   *G.6628(2)*

The exploitation of sources of precious metals was the
main objective of the Spanish conquerors in America
and the lure for later interlopers. After a preliminary
period of plunder, the Spanish began to mine gold and
silver ores systematically in both New Spain and Peru. A
dearth of native labour resulted in the establishment of a
slave trade importing negroes from Portuguese West
Africa to serve in the mines and elsewhere. This
lucrative trade lent itself to the activities of foreign
traders like John Hawkins, anxious to challenge the
Spanish and Portuguese monopolies.

In this stylized view, negro slaves are shown mining
gold in Hispaniola. The accompanying text is derived
from the popular work of the Milanese traveller,
Girolamo Benzoni, who sailed to see the New World in
1551. On his return in 1565 he wrote his *Historia del
Mondo Nuovo*, which formed the basis of Theodor de
Bry's own history illustrated here.

20 The silver mine at Potosí

Cerrode Potosi.
In: Pedro Lieca de Leon, *Parte Primera de la
Chronica del Peru*, Seville, 1553. f. cxxii verso.
30 cm   *983.g.18*

By 1550 gold had lost its importance as an export from
South America. Silver began to be mined in vast
quantities, first in the mines of New Spain and then, on
the discovery of mercury deposits at Huancavelica, from
the mine at Potosi in Upper Peru. By the 1570s over half
the export of American silver was produced at Potosi.

The large local mercury deposits at Huancavelica
were essential for the commercial extraction of the silver
from the mined ore. Mercury's characteristic fluidity
enabled it to amalgamate with molten silver easily, thus
separating the silver from surrounding ores.
Subsequently, the mixture of mercury and silver was
heated until the mercury vapourized, leaving the silver
to be cast into ingots. In this early woodcut view of the
'mountain of silver', the illustrator clearly regarded the
mine as a mixed blessing. On the hillside he has labelled
the various veins not only *de centeno*, the vein of a '100
reales', but also *veta de mendieta*, the vein of 'beggary'.

21 Sixteenth century Spanish and Mexican coinage

a ½ Real.   *55.2.16.81.*
b 2 Reales.   *SSB 145–138.*
c 8 Reales.   *C.0415.*
Lent by B.M. Department of Coins and Medals

Although much of the silver mined in New Spain and Peru was exported to Spain in bullion form, some of it was minted locally and supplied colonial needs for currency. The standard Spanish silver coin in the sixteenth century was the *real* which was worth 34 *maravedís*, the common accounting unit of Spanish money. A *real de a ocho* or a 'piece of eight', as it was popularly known in England, was therefore worth 272 *maravedís*. Treasure from America was expressed in terms of *pesos*; one *peso* equalled 450 *maravedís* worth of gold and silver. From 1560 to 1600 between 11 and 34 million *pesos* of silver and gold were exported annually to Spain. At that time the treasure would therefore have been worth about 2 to 7 million English pounds a year allowing for an exchange rate of 4 shillings to 1 peso; the rate quoted by the chronicler, Samuel Purchas.

The half-*real* piece, and the two-*real* piece were both minted in Mexico and bear the names of Charles V and Joanna on the obverse. On the reverse is a motif showing the mythical 'Pillars of Hercules', thought in classical times to stand either side of the Straits of Gibraltar. The *real de a ocho* was minted in Spain, at the height of American silver production, in 1584 and bears the arms and title of Philip II.

22 Keros from Peru

a Wooden *kero* or goblet with lacquer design showing a procession of men, some wearing Inca, and some European clothing.
Height 20.5 cm   *Lent by the Museum of Mankind, 1950 Am.22.1*

b Wooden *kero* or goblet with lacquer design showing two pairs of figures in Inca dress. In each case, the male figure holds a staff, and the female figure a flower. The cornucopia-like motif between the pairs of figures is a motif of the Colonial period showing European influence.
Height 19 cm *Lent by the Museum of Mankind 1950, Am.22.2*

c Small wooden *kero* or goblet with inlaid lacquer ornament. The geometric parts of the decoration are Inca in style, but the scene depicted shows men wearing European dress travelling in boats.
Height 14 cm *Lent by the Museum of Mankind, P.35*

The *kero* or goblet is one of the most typical wooden artefacts of the Inca period (*ca* AD 1200–1532) in Peru. Such vessels, conical in form, are frequently decorated with incised designs and elaborate inlaid lacquer decoration either geometric or figurative in content. The manufacture of *keros* continued well into the Colonial period following the Spanish Conquest; the style of the decoration often clearly shows the influence of European contact. The figurative scenes are an important source of information concerning Inca and Colonial period life.

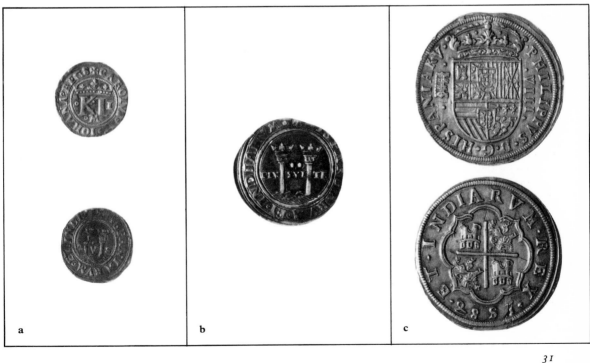

a   b   c   21

III

Drake's early career

THE chronicler, Edmund Howes, described Francis Drake as:

> 'Lowe of stature, of strong limbs, broade Breasted, round headed, browne hayre, full
> Bearded, his eyes rounde, Large and Cleare, well fauoured, fayre and of a cheerefull
> countenance.'

A number of contemporary representations of Drake survive, notably the miniature by
Nicholas Hilliard and the large engraved portrait by Jodocus Hondius (see **107, 24** respectively).
Little can be said with assurance about his birth, parentage and early life. He was born probably
near South Tavistock, Devon, about 1540. He had at least three brothers, all sailors: John and
Joseph, who died in the West Indies in 1572–3, and Thomas, who outlived them all. They were
kinsmen of John Hawkins.

It is very likely that Drake's early experience of the sea was in the coasting trade. His first
recorded voyage was with Captain John Lovell in 1566 to the West Indies; Lovell hoped to
emulate John Hawkins's successes of 1562 and 1564 in breaking the Spanish monopoly of trade
in the West Indies. He was outwitted, however, by Miguel de Castellanos, the Spanish governor
at Rio de la Hacha on the Spanish Main. Castellanos 'bought' slaves brought from West Africa
by Lovell and then refused to pay for them. It was said that this experience of Spanish treachery
coloured Drake's subsequent attitude towards Spain. Drake's dealings with the Spanish in his
next voyage were even more unfortunate. This time he sailed in 1567 from Plymouth with John
Hawkins; Queen Elizabeth I lent her naval vessel, the *Jesus of Lübeck*, for the enterprise. In
September 1568 the Spanish attacked the English, in breach of a truce, at San Juan de Ulúa (now
Vera Cruz). Hawkins lost the *Jesus* and all his other ships except the *Minion*, which he
commanded himself, and the *Judith*, captained by Drake. Drake arrived back in Plymouth in
January 1569 ahead of Hawkins, whose elder brother, William, promptly sent him to tell his tale
at court to Sir William Cecil (1520–1598), later first Lord Burghley, the Queen's principal
Secretary of State. This was probably Drake's first contact with the court. Whilst on shore he
married his first wife, Mary Newman, on 4 July 1569 at St Budeaux parish church near
Plymouth. Drake may have visited the Caribbean in 1570 and 1571 in search of information,
observing coasts and harbours, capturing Spaniards and cross-examining them about Spanish
settlements and garrisons, and in particular about Nombre de Dios in Panama.

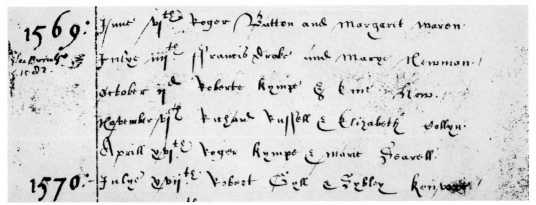

A 1610 transcript of the first St Budeaux register showing the entry for Drake's marriage to Mary Newman on 4 July 1569 (from *Devon Record Office*).

In May 1572 he set sail from Plymouth with his brothers John and Joseph, and John Oxenham, for Nombre de Dios. He planned to attack the store-house where Spaniards kept the bullion and precious stones they had taken from Peru, before shipping them in armed convoy to Spain. Richard Hakluyt's account of this raid was translated from the Portuguese of 'one Lopez Vas' and is short and garbled. William Camden's version, though brief, contains all the essentials, while the longest and liveliest accounts are to be found in Sloane MS 301 and *Sir Francis Drake revived* (1626). Briefly, Drake made an unsuccessful attack on Nombre de Dios, withdrew, and spent some months marauding along the Main. Then, allying himself with the Cimaroons, he ambushed a treasure train near Nombre de Dios and returned to England with £40,000 in Spanish silver. In the course of this expedition he is said to have caught his first sight of the Pacific and made his vow to navigate it.

On his triumphant return on 9 August 1573, Drake, 'now growne abundantly rich', according to Camden, found the government trying to restore good relations with Spain and so, prudently, he vanished from the public scene. He is next recorded in 1575 serving under the first Earl of Essex in Ireland, where he made the acquaintance of Thomas Doughty who was to achieve notoriety during Drake's 'Famous Voyage'.

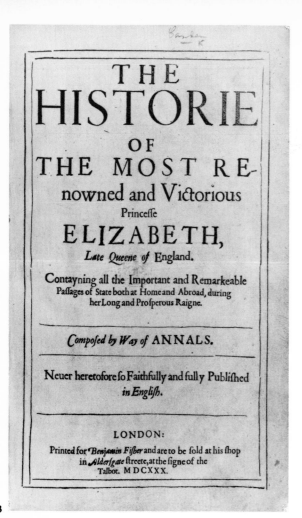

upon the Riuer Medway, (where the fleet lyeth at anchor).

It is not very likely that Drake provided Camden with this information. Facts about Drake's origins and early life are difficult to obtain. It is possible, as Camden asserts, that Francis Russell, 2nd Earl of Bedford (1527–1585) was Drake's godfather. John Russell, 1st Earl of Bedford, acquired the town and Abbey of Tavistock, Devon, in 1539 and Drake was born, probably near Tavistock, about the year 1540. In his continuation (1615) of John Stow's *Chronicles* (1580), Edmund Howes stated that the first name of Drake's father was 'Edmond'. The Subsidy Roll for 1544 records an Edmund Drake as living in the parish of Tavistock. He may have been Drake's father. This Edmund, a 'sherman', was indicted in 1548 for stealing a horse, assaulting a 'Roger Langisforde' and stealing '21s 7d which he had in his purse'. He seems to have fled the district, though he was subsequently granted a pardon. These circumstances, taken with Camden's account, have led historians to believe that Edmund quitted the county, gave people to understand that he had fled from Devon in order to avoid religious persecution and, early in Elizabeth's reign, became vicar of Upchurch (not Upnor) in Kent.

An Edmund Drake was vicar of Upchurch, on the Medway, five miles south-east of Chatham and the naval dockyard, from 1560 until his death, but it seems unlikely that he was the same person as the Tavistock Edmund, or the father of Francis Drake. His will dated 26 December 1566, and proved on 16 January 1567, does not mention a son Francis, or a John or a Joseph, but only an Edward and a Thomas.

23 His family

The Historie of the Most Renowned and Victorious Princesse Elizabeth . . . Composed by Way of Annals . . . Neuer heretofore so Faithfully and fully Published in English. London. Printed for Benjamin Fisher . . . 1630. Booke 2, pp. 110–111. 28 cm   *10805. f. 18*

William Camden (1551–1623), in this English edition of his *Annales* wrote:

This Drake (to relate no more than what I haue heard from himselfe) was borne of meane parentage in Devonshire, and had Francis Russell (afterwards Earle of Bedford) to his Godfather . . . Whilest hee was yet a child, his Father imbracing the Protestants Doctrine . . . fled his Countrey, and withdrew himselfe into Kent . . . hee got a place among the Saylors in the Kings fleet, to reade prayers vnto them: and soone after was ordained Deacon, and made Vicar of the Church of Upnore

25

24 Francis Drake (1540?–1596)

Franciscus Draeck nobilissimus eques angliae an. aet. sue 43.
Engraved portrait, three-quarter length.
[London, Jodocus Hondius?, second state.]
39 × 31 cm *Lent by B.M. Department of Prints and Drawings, Cracherode O.8–87*

According to the inscription in the lower margin this is a portrait of Drake 'from the life' at the age of forty-three. In the eighteenth century the engraver and antiquary George Vertue attributed this portrait to Jodocus Hondius, the Flemish engraver, who was at work in London in the early 1590s. Vertue acquired the plate at some point and probably retouched it before issuing the present impression.

25 Plymouth and the south-west coast

Plymouth, its estuary, and the country and coast to the west, *ca* 1536.
MS colour on vellum 73 × 82 cm *Cotton MS Augustus I. i. 38*

This attractive manuscript is part of a large chart and bird's eye view of the coast and hinterland of England from Land's End to Exmouth (Cotton MS Augustus I, i, 35, 36, 38, 39). It is one of the earliest extant English charts made for sailors. The features that mariners would need to look out for have been marked and brought into prominence by a foreshortening of the depth and protraction of the width of the area surveyed.

Plymouth was one of the most important ports in Elizabethan England and played a large part in Drake's career. It was the home town of John and William Hawkins; their father, William, had been mayor and member of parliament for Plymouth; Drake himself was mayor in 1581. Tavistock, where Drake was probably born, is also clearly marked. As his home port, Plymouth was Drake's usual point of departure for all his notable expeditions including the circumnavigation of 1577–80.

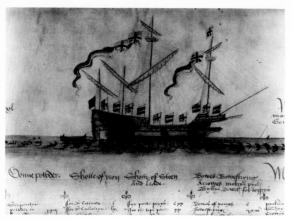

26 i The *Swallowe* (detail from Additional MS 22047, The second Rolle . . . of the Kynges . . . Galliasses (no. 26).

26 Henry VIII's navy

'The second Rolle declarying The Nombre of the Kynges Majestys owne Galliasses.'
MS vellum roll 509 × 82 cm
Additional MS 22047

One of three vellum rolls describing and illustrating the King's Navy, this manuscript bears the name of Anthony Anthony, one of the officers of the Ordnance, and was presented to Henry VIII in 1546. It contains coloured drawings of the royal galliasses (low-built vessels, larger than galleys, impelled by both sail and oars and chiefly employed in war); descriptions of the tonnage of the ships, the number of crew, both 'gonnars' and 'marrynars', required to man them; and of the 'Ordenaunce', 'artillary', 'municions' and 'habilliments for the warre'. The two companion rolls were given to Samuel Pepys, Secretary to the Admiralty, by Charles II in 1680. Pepys's rolls were cut up and bound into a large volume and placed in his library, which he left to Magdalene College, Cambridge. One of the ships, the *Jesus of Lübeck*, drawn in the Pepys manuscript, is illustrated. Henry VIII had bought the *Jesus* from the Hanseatic League in 1544; Queen Elizabeth I lent it to John Hawkins in 1564, and again in 1567–8 when he sailed to the West Indies with Drake. On this second voyage Hawkins was obliged to abandon the ship at San Juan de Ulúa when attacked by the Spanish. Not until the late 1570s, under the supervision of John Hawkins, were new ships like the *Revenge* and *Ark Royal* built; these were to play a large part in defeating the Spanish Armada in 1588.

26 ii The *Jesus of Lübeck*, detail from Pepys MS 2991, (Pepys Library, Magdalene College, Cambridge).

27 San Juan de Ulúa

a View and ground plan of this fortress by Cristóbal de Eraso, *ca* 1570.
Ink with some water colouring. Vellum.
52 × 72 cm   *Lent by Hans P. Kraus*

This and the next item are the earliest extant American military architectural drawings. San Juan de Ulúa in New Spain was the centre for Spanish-Mexican trade and communications. In 1570, the fortress at San Juan de Ulúa 'consisted of a tower, with embrasures for artillery and a gun-platform on the top, and a stone wall 300 feet in length along the shore. Ships were moored to the wall by means of hawsers passed through the large iron rings shown here.' Shown in this view are the proposed additions: a 138-foot extension of the wall, and a large tower with two gun platforms. (Hans P. Kraus *Sir Francis Drake* (1970) p. 211.) These additions, planned to strengthen the fortress, were obviously thought necessary because of the engagement between the Spanish and John Hawkins and Francis Drake in September 1568. In October 1567 Hawkins had sailed from Plymouth with the *Jesus of Lübeck*, the *Minion* and several smaller vessels, one of which, the *Judith*, Drake came to command in the course of the voyage. The professed object of the voyage was the buying of slaves in Guinea which were then to be taken to the West Indies and sold. A cargo of negro slaves was procured, the West Indies reached, and by August 1568 most of the slaves had been sold; but then bad weather so damaged the *Jesus* that Hawkins was obliged to look for shelter in order to make repairs.

He put into the harbour of San Juan de Ulúa in September, but two days later the annual convoy from Spain with the new Viceroy of New Spain, Don Martin Enriquez de Almansa, on board, came into view. Hawkins concluded a truce with Enriquez, allowing the Viceroy to enter San Juan providing that Hawkins's fleet was left unmolested. All of Hawkins's ships, and part of the Spanish fleet, were moored side by side with their bows to the sea-wall and fort depicted in the plan when the Spanish broke the agreement and attacked the English, driving them from the bay with a great loss of men and ships, including the *Jesus*.

b Ground Plan of a projected fortress by Cristóbal de Eraso, *ca* 1570.
Ink, with part in yellow water colour. Vellum.
71 × 64 cm   *Lent by Hans P. Kraus*

The portion of the plan (part of a tower and one wall) in yellow colouring displays the San Juan fortification as it was at the time of the battle between the Spaniards and John Hawkins in 1568.

c *A true declaration of the troublesome voyadge of M. John Haukins . . . in . . . 1567 and 1568.*
Imprinted for Lucas Harrison, London, 1569.
(sig. Biiij verso.)
13 cm   *C.32.a.16.*

In this account of his 1567–8 adventures Hawkins relates how at San Juan de Ulúa 'wyth the Minion onelye and the Judith (a small barke of 50 tonne) we escaped which barke the same nighte forsoke us in oure great miserie.' The passage implies that Drake left Hawkins to take his chance in the unwieldy larger ship and made good his escape to England. Nothing certain is known about Drake's movements between his parting from Hawkins at San Juan in September 1568 and his reappearance in Plymouth in January 1569.

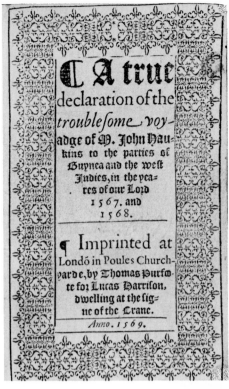

¶ A true
declaration of the
troublesome voy-
adge of M. John Hau-
kins to the parties of
Guynea and the west
Indies, in the yea-
res of our Lord
1567. and
1568.

¶ Imprinted at
Londó in Poules Church-
yarde, by Thomas Purfo-
te for Lucas Harrison,
dwelling at the sig-
ne of the Crane.
Anno. 1569.

27c

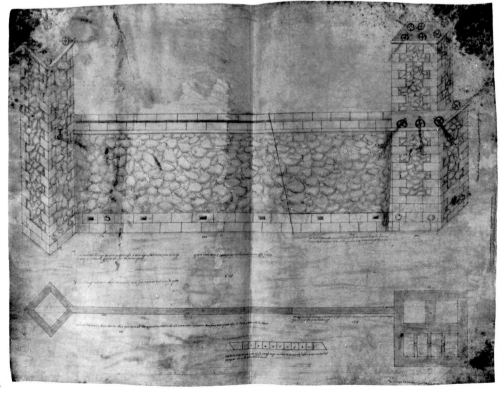

27a

Qui *bicit toties inp* frut*fis claffibus boftis*
Jlle bagis HAWKINS *bitam relliquit in bndis*

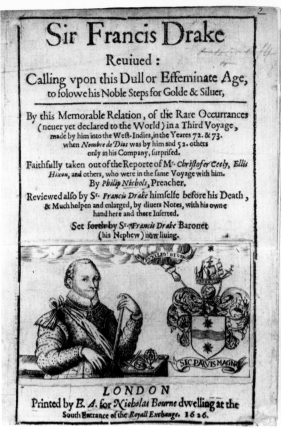

Sir Francis Drake

Reuiued :

Calling vpon this Dull or Effeminate Age,
to folowe his Noble Steps for Golde & Siluer,

By this Memorable Relation, of the Rare Occurrances
(neuer yet declared to the World) in a Third Voyage,
made by him into the Weſt-Indies, in the Yeares 72. & 73.
when *Nombre de Dios* was by him and 52. others
only in his Company, furprifed.

Faithfully taken out of the Reporte of M.ʳ *Chriſtofer Ceely*, *Ellis
Hixon*, and others, who were in the fame Voyage with him.
By *Philip Nichols*, Preacher.

Reviewed alfo by S.ʳ *Francis Drake* himſelfe before his Death,
& Much holpen and enlarged, by diuers Notes, with his owne
hand here and there Inſerted.

Set forth by S.ʳ *Francis Drake* Baronet
(his Nephew) now liuing.

LONDON
Printed by E. A. for *Nicholas Bourne* dwelling at the
South Entrance of the *Royall Exchange*. 1626.

28 Drake and the Court

William Hawkins to Sir William Cecil, 20 January
1568/9.
MS 31 × 23 cm

Lent by the P.R.O.; S.P. 12/49 no. 36.

Having escaped in the *Judith* from the Spaniards at San
Juan de Ulúa, Drake arrived back in Plymouth on 20
January 1569. William, John Hawkins's elder brother,
worried by Drake's account of the Spanish treachery at
San Juan and the continued absence of his brother sent
'. . . the Capetayne [of the *Judith*] . . . beynge our
kynsman, callyd fransyes dracke' to Sir William Cecil
'Chefe Secretary' to the Queen to give an account of his
experiences, that '. . . the Quenes maieste may be
advertesyd of the same'. This was probably Drake's first
contact with the Court. Five days after this letter was
written John Hawkins anchored the *Minion*, the other
surviving vessel, in Mount's Bay.

The illustration of John Hawkins is from Henry
Holland's *Herwologia*, 1620.

29 Drake in the West Indies 1572–3

'A Relation of the rare occurrences in a third
voyage made by Sir Francis Drake into the West
Indies in the years 72 and 73 . . . by Phillip
Nicholls Preacher.'
28 × 19 cm   *Sloane MS 301*, f. 25.

In May 1572 Drake set sail from Plymouth with his
brothers John and Joseph and John Oxenham. He was
heading for Nombre de Dios in Panama, possibly
seeking revenge for the humiliation he had suffered at
the hands of the Spanish at San Juan de Ulúa in 1568.
Precious stones, gold and silver from Peru were shipped
by the Spaniards along the west coast of South America
to the town of Panama in the Pacific, and then carried
across the Isthmus by pack-mules to Nombre de Dios.
Less valuable and bulkier goods were sent down the
river Chagres to the Atlantic coast near Nombre de
Dios. Between Panama and Nombre de Dios on the
Chagres was the small river port and settlement of Venta
Cruces. At Nombre de Dios there was a storehouse to
which the treasure was brought to be shipped in the
'galleones' to Spain. Drake's plan was to attack this
treasure-house. He made a successful attack on Nombre
de Dios in July 1572, but a tropical storm, and injuries to

some of his crew and himself, forced him to retire empty-handed. He then spent several months prowling about the Spanish Main, caught his first sight of the Pacific, and finally in 1573 successfully attacked a train of pack-mules carrying gold and silver to Nombre de Dios.

The folio exhibited describes his successful attack on the 'recoes'; 'reco' is a corruption of the Spanish 'recua' meaning a drove of beasts of burden, the beasts in question being 'moiles' *i.e.* mules. The 'French Captaine' mentioned in the extract was Le Testu, a Huguenot Captain from Le Havre whom the Spaniards captured. Having achieved the purpose of his expedition Drake made good his escape to England.

30   Drake sees the Pacific

Sir Francis Drake Reuiued . . . the Rare Occurrances in a . . . Voyage, made by him into the West-Indies, in the Yeares 72 & 73 . . . by Philip Nichols, Preacher. London, Printed for Nicholas Bourne, 1626. pp. 58–9.
20 cm   *C.32.e.29*

This book purports to relate 'Occurrances neuer yet declared to the World . . . Faithfully taken out of the Reporte of Mr. Christofer Ceely, Ellis Hixon, and others', who accompanied Drake in his voyage and claims to have been 'Reviewed also by Sir Francis Drake himselfe before his Death, and Much holpen and enlarged, by diuers Notes with his owne hand here and there Inserted'. It is 'Set forth by Sr Francis Drake Baronet (his Nephew) now liuing'. It is obviously related to Sloane MS 301. Despite its lively and colourful style the work has some merit insofar as its details are confirmed by contemporary Spanish documents. It is certainly a vivid account of Drake's exploits. The pages exhibited tell how Drake, in the Isthmus of Panama in 1573, joined forces with the 'Symerons' or Cimaroons (a mixed tribe of Indians and runaway negro slaves who inhabited the inaccessible interior of this the narrowest part of America) and climbed a 'goodly and great high Tree' and saw 'th' Atlantick Ocean whence now wee came, and the South Atlantick so much desired' and 'besought Almighty God of his goodnes, to give him life and leaue to sayle once in an English Ship in that Sea; and then calling vp all the rest of our men, acquainted Iohn Oxnam especially with this his peticion and purpose,' that was, to sail the Pacific.

IV

Plans for the voyage 1577

MUCH of the preparation and planning of Drake's South Sea voyage has been obscured by the secrecy required to hoodwink the Spanish. Although suspect, Drake's intentions remained safe. As late as 31 March 1578, the Spanish ambassador, Mendoza, wrote that he had heard that some six weeks before Christmas, Drake had left with four or five ships for Nombre de Dios in the West Indies. Drake may have been contemplating the voyage as early as 1575, as Thomas Doughty his companion in Ireland and on the voyage was later heard to assert. By mid-1577 plans were well advanced. The Queen was informed and, despite the warlike implications of a voyage to the Pacific by heavily armed ships under the command of Drake, she evidently approved the scheme. Significantly perhaps, Lord Burghley, an advocate of maintaining the peace with England's traditional ally Spain, was apparently not informed about the voyage; although Doughty later admitted that he had given Burghley details of the project. Once at sea a number of additional possibilities were evidently discussed, including going for the Moluccas, and searching for a return route through the strait of Anian. In the event Drake used his discretion to 'make' the voyage and return safely by the Cape of Good Hope.

The fleet of five ships which set out from Plymouth 13 December 1577 was supposedly provisioned for eighteen to twenty months with the usual ship's diet; biscuit, beer, wine, salted beef, pork, oil and salt. Evidently, however, the agent James Sydye had not provided adequate food for the fleet, and the stores were replenished from Spanish and Portuguese ships captured on the voyage to the Cape Verde islands. A brief description of the English fleet was given by John Drake in his deposition to the Inquisition on 24 March 1584. A fuller one of the *Pelican* was made by the captured pilot Nuño da Silva: 'The *Capitana* [*i.e. Pelican*] is in a great measure stout and strong. She is fit for warfare and of the French build, well fitted out with very good masts, tackle and double sails. She is a good sailer and the rudder governs her well . . . She has seven armed potholes on each side, and inside she carries eighteen pieces of artillery . . . also an abundance of all sorts of amunition for war.' The gunners aboard also manufactured various ingenious fire devices and cannon shot while a smith, complete with forge, made nails, bolts and spikes.

Also carried on board were the usual complement of navigational instruments and a number of published works on navigation. The only clue to their identity is to be found in the sworn deposition made by the reluctant Portuguese pilot, Nuño da Silva, to the Mexican Inquisition

31 Drake's tide-tables (from Pepys Library, Magdalene College, Cambridge).

concerning his captivity on board Drake's flag-ship, the *Golden Hind*. Da Silva recorded that 'Drake carried with him three books on navigation. One of these was in French, another in English. The third was Magellan's 'Discovery'; in what language this was, deponeth knoweth not.' A number of books have been suggested as possibilities for Drake's library on board, including those which are described below.

31 The art of navigation

a *The Arte of Navigation, Conteynyng a compendious description of the Sphere, with the makyng of certen Instrumentes and Rules for Navigations . . . by Martin Curtes.* Translated out of Spanyshe into Englyshe by Richard Eden. London, 1561. The 3 part, f. lix.
18 cm   G. 7310

The first navigation manual to be printed in English was a translation of Martin Cortés's book published in Seville in 1551. Divided into three parts, the book first discusses the earth and universe from a Ptolemaic standpoint, and then turns to the use of instruments to determine the course of the sun, the moon and the stars. Sun-dials and nocturnals, tide-tables and finally weather lore are considered for the navigator's benefit. The familiar rule of 'red sky at night' is explained thus: 'the redde colour which appeareth in the evenyng, signifieth the dryenesse of the ayre: whereby the matter of the grosse vapours which should be co[n]verted into water, is so muche dried, that it appeareth in manner inflamed, and is therefore redde . . . And is therefore the nearest sygne of fayre weather.' The third part deals exclusively with navigation; in particular, precise instructions are given for constructing the sea card or chart, with explanatory diagrams showing a bar or linear scale and a latitude scale (f. lix). The compass, the cross-staff, and the astrolabe are then described, often by working paper models (volvelles) attached to the appropriate page. Cortés's manual of instruction continued to be published in English until 1630.

b [A chart of the Atlantic coasts of Europe, North Africa, and North and Central America.] Par N. Nicolaj du dauphine Geographe du Roy.
In: *L'Art de naviguer de maistre Pierre de Medine, Espaignol . . . Traduict . . . . par Nicolas de Nicolaj, du Dauphiné . . .* Lyon, 1554.
35 × 42 cm   C.54.i.3

The French manual on navigation which Nuño da Silva saw on board the *Golden Hind* is generally thought to have been a translation of Pedro Medina's *Arte de Navegar*, 1545. The work was not translated into English until 1581, but it includes very clear instructions on how to find latitude by the sun or the stars; these are accompanied by simple diagrams. Nicolas de Nicolai, formerly in the service of Henry VIII as a hydrographer and pilot, later became Cosmographer to King Henri II of France to whom this work was dedicated in 1554.

c 'A briefe declaration of the viage or navigation made about the Worlde. Geathered out of a large booke written hereof by Master Antoni Pigafetta . . . one of the compagnie of that vyage in the which Ferdinando Magalianes a Portugale . . . was

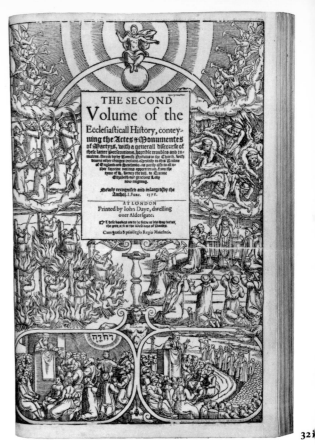

generall captayne of the navie.'
In: *The History of Trauayle in the West and East Indies . . . by Richard Eden . . . and finished by Richarde Willes.* London, 1577. pp. 431ᵛ–448.
19 cm   304.d.10

The third work Nuño da Silva noted on Drake's ship was Magellan's 'Discovery'. Da Silva was unable to say what language the work was written in, and as he evidently knew French and English, the book in question is generally assumed to be the Latin edition of Maximulanus Transylvanus' *De Moluccis Insulis*, first published in 1523, which describes Magellan's voyage in some detail. If on the other hand da Silva had not actually seen the books or had only glimpsed them (which may indeed be the fact as his answers are so uncertain) the account may well have been an English translation of Magellan's voyage as written by one of his company, Antonio Pigafetta. Such a translation by Richard Eden and augmented by Richard Willes had been printed in London in 1577.

Certainly John Wynter carried an English translation of Magellan's *Voyage* on board. At the end of October 1578, in the Strait of Magellan, he read some passages from it to his ship's master and company in an abortive effort to persuade them to continue to the Moluccas.

IOHANNES FOXVS.
Colligit ut FOXVS Sanctorum gesta virorum
Digna facit Sanctis plurima martyribus.
Æ

32 Protestant instruction on board

*The Second Volume of the Ecclesiasticall History,
conteyning the Actes & Monumentes of Martyrs . . .
by I. Foxe.* London, 1576.
35 cm   *C.15.c.8*

Both the Portuguese pilot, Nuño da Silva and Gomez
Rengifo, a Spanish shipper captured by Drake at
Guatulco on 13 April 1579, record Drake's custom of
holding religious services on board, where he himself
read the psalms and preached to the company. On
examination by the Mexican Inquisition, Gomez
Rengifo described one such service where Drake
evidently also read from an edition of John Foxe's *Book
of Martyrs*. He showed the book to the Spaniard,
pointing out the dramatic woodcut illustrations of
Protestants burning at the stake which, he said,
represented those 'who had been martyred and burnt in
Castile'.

In 1571 Convocation had directed that copies of
Foxe's *Book of Martyrs* be placed in cathedrals in
England and Wales, and no doubt an ardent Protestant
like Drake recognized the *Book's* value in his battle
against the Spanish. The title-page to the two volume
work illustrates the 'Persecuted' or Protestant church in
contrast to the 'Persecuting' or Roman Catholic church.

The people of God's word and of the Bible are
juxtaposed with the ceremonious 'rosary telling'
Catholics, whose ultimate destination in Hell is
depicted.

Drake was a personal friend of John Foxe, for a
contemporary copy of a letter sent by Francis Drake to a
'Mr. Foxe, preacher' is preserved in the Harleian
manuscripts (MS 167 f. 104). 'Written by the hands of
M. Pynner' during the Cadiz campaign in April 1587 the
letter concludes 'your loving freende and faythfull sonne
in Christ Jesus, Francis Drake'. The letter was printed
in *The true and perfecte Newes of the woorthy and valiaunt
exploytes . . . doone by . . . Syr Frauncis Drake, 1587*
written by Thomas Greepe immediately after the Cadiz
campaign.

33 Drake reads the psalms

*The Whole Booke of Psalmes, collected into Englishe
Metre by Thom. Sternh. John Hopkins and others.*
London, 1576.
19 cm   *3434.e.45*

Several attempts were made in the first half of the
sixteenth century to provide a rhyming, metrical
translation of the Psalms for congregational singing in
church. Amongst them was a small selection made by
Thomas Sternhold and published, without music, in
1549, the year of his death. A larger selection was
published in Geneva in 1556 for the use of the
Protestants who had taken refuge there. The tunes
included in this edition became immediately popular –
some, such as the Old 100th, are still sung today – and
the complete book of Psalms by Sternhold, Hopkins and
others, first published in 1562, became the Authorized
Version. Thereafter editions were published almost
yearly, and although its popularity waned in the mid-
seventeenth century it continued to appear until the
second decade of the nineteenth century. This version is
probably the one taken by Drake on his voyage.

34 Navigational instruments

a   English lodestone, unsigned. 17th century.
A brass-bound lodestone with steel keep-plate and
suspension ring. Decorated with a circular silver
mount. Weight 800 grams.
7 × 7 × 4 cm   *Lent by Harriet Wynter Ltd*

Before the eighteenth century the only way of
magnetizing a compass needle was by 'touching' it with a
lodestone. An oxide of iron, lodestone exhibits magnetic
properties in its natural state and will transfer these to
other metals. Lodestones were taken to sea on long
voyages to 'refresh' the soft iron wires of the compass
needle and were kept magnetic by the use of an iron

by Sir Francis Drake to Lawrence Keymis, Sir Walter Raleigh's collaborator in his Guiana voyages, is now in the collection of Baroness Wharton.

b A wooden cross-staff.
A replica of the instrument originally made in ivory by Thomas Tuttell *ca* 1700.
786 mm   *Lent by Harriet Wynter Ltd*

The cross-staff is said to have been invented by Levi ben Gerson in 1342, and it remained in common use well into the seventeenth century and later. It was used by the seaman to take the altitude of the sun or a star above the horizon so that he might calculate his latitude. Usually made of wood, about thirty inches long, the cross-staff was a four-sided rod; each side about $\frac{1}{2}$ inch wide, on which were engraved scales of degrees from 0° to 90°, which were to be read when the cross-piece was correctly aligned. In the late sixteenth century a second cross-piece was employed to allow greater flexibility in taking accurate sights.

34(c) Detail from *The Seaman's Secrets*, 1595.

34a

keep-plate or keeper (in the upper illustration) which was held to the two protruding magnetic ends of the lodestone by the lodestone's own magnetism. The keeper also protected the compass needle from the effect of 'deviation' which a naked magnet would induce in the needle if taken near the compass. To 'refresh' the needle the keeper was removed and the magnet was stroked across it.

A lodestone in a silver mount, said to have been given

34b

34d

34e

Using the cross-staff

c   *The Seaman's Secrets, devided into 2 partes, wherein is taught the three kindes of Sayling, Horizontal, Perodoxall [sic], and sayling upon a great Circle . . . by Iohn Davis.* London, 1595.
21 cm   *C.54.bb.33*

The cross-staff was placed to the eye and the cross-piece was then moved up and down the shaft until its lower end was aligned with the horizon. At the same time the upper edge was aligned with the bottom of the sun. To increase accuracy a second longer cross-piece was sometimes added and aligned in the same way. This method is well illustrated and described in John Davis's *The Seaman's Secrets* (1595) where he instructs the navigator in computing his altitude or latitude. The angular distance of the sun from the horizon is read from the cross-staff's scale and then subtracted from 90° to obtain the distance of the sun from the observer's zenith. By referring to the seaman's regiment or tables of the sun's declination for the particular time of the year, and then adding or subtracting the sun's declination, the ship's actual latitude could be obtained.

d   A pair of bronze dividers. German, 16th century.
Height 28 cm *Lent by B.M. Department of Medieval and Later Antiquities 1903, 2-28, 1.*

The oldest plotting instrument was undoubtedly a pair

of dividers. These were used for pricking off the ship's course on a chart and for measuring distances against the calibrations of the linear or bar scale. In the sixteenth century dividers were more commonly called compasses and, together with a simple rule, they formed the equipment necessary for navigating with a plane chart.

e   Mariner's astrolabe. Scales of limb 90–0, 0–90.
Weight (1870 gm); diam: 184 mm.
Lent by the Museum of the History of Science, Oxford

Developed during the late fifteenth and early sixteenth centuries by the Portuguese, the mariner's astrolabe of cast brass was designed specifically for taking altitude measurements at sea of the sun with a view to determining the ship's latitude. To measure the altitude of the sun, the astrolabe was usually held at waist height by its suspension ring, and turned until it pointed towards the sun. The alidade (or vane) was then rotated until a spot of sunlight passing through the pinnule (or pin-hole) of the upper vane fell exactly through the pinnule of the lower vane. The altitude was then read off at the point where the edge or point of the alidade cut the degree scale. An early illustration of the mariner's astrolabe was published by Pedro de Medina in his *Regimento de Navegacion*, 1563.

As the sixteenth century progressed the mariner's astrolabe was developed to improve its accuracy and ease of use. The weight of the instrument was distributed so

45

that the bottom was heavier than the top to counteract the movement of the ship which interfered with the astrolabe's vertical suspension; the alidade points were made less blunt and the calibrations of the degree scales finer; zenith distances as well as altitudes could also be read from the scales. Even so the astrolabe was gradually supplanted during the seventeenth century by the more accurate wooden cross-staff which was progressively improved in the sixteenth century, culminating in the invention of the back-staff by Captain John Davis in the 1590s.

f A mariner's compass. Italian (?); late 16th century. Diam. 108 mm (A photograph) *National Maritime Museum C.82/52–126*

Probably the oldest surviving compass in Europe, this dry-card compass is mounted with gimbals in an ivory bowl. The card is graduated to thirty-two points with the north point decorated by a *fleur de lys*. By the fifteenth century confidence in the magnetic compass was such that it was used universally to find direction at sea. The compass 'wire' or needle was a length of soft iron wire, bent double into a loop and pinched at each end to equal the diameter of the compass card; the wire was then stuck on to the underside of the card, aligned from the north to the south point. The wire and card were then placed on a brass cone or 'capital' on which the wired card could pivot freely. The compass was mounted in two brass gimbals which moved with each other in such a way that the compass remained level despite the movement of the ship.

35 'Drake's dial'

A compendium, signed 'Humfray Colle made this diall anno 1569'.
Brass gilt; diam: 63 × 56 mm *Lent by the National Maritime Museum, Greenwich Hospital Collection*

Reputedly this compendium once belonged to Francis Drake, but its provenance cannot be traced with any certainty earlier than 1812, when it passed into the hands of Robert Bigsby of Sion-hill House, Nottinghamshire. His son then presented the dial to King William IV, who deposited it in the Greenwich Hospital collection in 1831. Known as 'Drake's dial' for the last 150 years, the compendium is one of the earliest English-made dials to be preserved, and was made by the Elizabethan scientific instrument-maker and engraver, Humfray Cole (fl. *ca* 1568–91), who held the office of 'sinker of stamps' at the Royal Mint until his death in 1591. The pocket-sized instrument, which is derived from Leonard Digges's *Prognostication* of 1555, includes a universal equinoctial dial; a table of latitudes of places in the British Isles and Europe; a tide table for the principal ports in Europe giving the moon's bearing or time of high water at each, with an accompanying dial to calculate 'the ebb[es] [a]nd fluddes'; a dial showing the moon's phases; a perpetual calendar giving the dates of movable feastdays; and a circumferentor for taking horizontal angular sights which could also be suspended vertically and used as an astrolabe. This last was called 'The Geometricall Square' by Humfray Cole and seems to be based on Leonard Digges's seminal surveying work, the *Tectonicon*, 1556.

34f

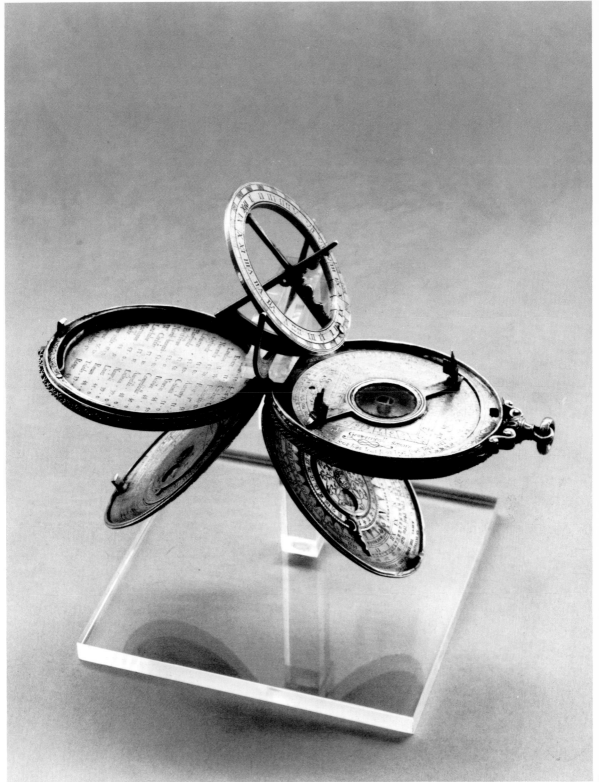

36 The sailor's attire

Del marinaro Inglese. In: *Habiti Antichi et Moderni di tutto il Mondo di Cesare Vecellio.* Venetia, 1598. p. 282
18 cm   *143.a.11*

A contemporary Italian illustration of a sixteenth century English sailor's attire. The accompanying text in Italian and Latin, describes the clothes as follows: 'Their clothes are of wool, yellowish-red and white. The cloak is short, the breeches longish, wide, baggy and full of folds. The hat is shaggy and made of felt.'

The common sailor however would probably have worn a plain leather jerkin over his shirt and less baggy trousers, more in keeping with his duties. An illustration of a sailor handling a log-line, and dressed more simply, forms part of the title-page illustration to Willem Janszoon Blaeu's *Licht der Zee-vaert*, 1608.

37 Planning the Voyage

A MS memorandum giving some account of the proposed expedition by Francis Drake to the Pacific Ocean, *ca* 1577.
31 cm   *Cotton MS Otho E. VIII f. 8–9*

This manuscript memorandum, presumably set down for Walsingham to present the case for Drake's voyage to the Queen in 1577, is included in a volume containing a number of letters and papers relating to English voyages *ca* 1553–1610. As the document has been badly charred

37 i Sir Christopher Hatton (Reproduced by kind permission of the National Portrait Gallery).

36

its interpretation has been the subject of controversy since its discovery by E. G. R. Taylor in 1929.

The first page (f. 8) refers to Drake's bark *The Francis* and to six pinnaces which were to be carried in it, presumably for reconnoitring inshore, and then lists the provisions and equipment necessary for the voyage, including £50 as 'presentes to be given to the Ll. [*i.e.* Lords] of The Cowmptres [*i.e.* countries] of dyvers sortes'. The second page (illustrated) lists the proposed backers of the voyage, who were the Lord Admiral of England, the Earl of Lincoln; Sir William Wynter, Surveyor of the Navy; his brother George Wynter, Clerk of the Queen's Ships; and John Hawkins, Drake's cousin. From the Queen's immediate circle came three other promoters: the Earl of Leicester, her favourite and a Privy Councillor; Sir Francis Walsingham, Secretary of State; and Sir Christopher Hatton, Captain of the Queen's Bodyguard. Drake himself invested £1,000 in the voyage which he no doubt expected to regain with interest. Then begins the memorandum, perhaps set down after a preliminary meeting of the promoters. Walsingham is asked to see whether the Queen will lend her ship the *Swallow* for the enterprise, and to make sure that she is 'mayde pryve to the trewth of the viage, and yet the coollor [*i.e.* colour] to be geven owt for allixandria'.

It is evident from this, and from an estimate drawn up by John Hawkins in June 1577, that the voyage to Alexandria by the *Swallow* and the *Pelican* was an elaborate cover to confuse the Spanish about the objectives of the plan. As much of the writing is now lost through fire, and the fragment remaining is ambiguous especially with regard to the ultimate destination of the ships, the full text of the passage is given below:

> 'the powlle/the sowthe sea then/far to the northwards as/along the saied coaste/as of the other to fynde owt/to have trafiek for the vent/of thies her Mat^ties Realmes,/they ar not under the obediens of/prynces, so is ther great hoepe of/spieces, drugs, cochynille, and/speciall comodities, such as maye/her highnes domynyons, and also/shipping awoork greatly and/gotten up as aforesaid in to XXX de[grees]/the southe sea(yf it shall be thowght/by the fore named frances draek/to/far) then he is to retorne the same way/whome [home] words, as he went owt wch viage/by godes favor is to be performed in XIIth month./All thowghe he shuld spend V monthes in/taryenge uppon the coaste to get knowle[dge]/of the prynces and cowmptres [countries] ther.'

A further note presses the point that the Queen must give an answer with all possible speed or the voyage 'cannot take the good affect, as is hoepped for'. Presumably the plans might become known and the element of surprise and security lost.

The objective of the voyage, as conceived when the memorandum was drawn up, seems to have been to sail to the Pacific Ocean through the Magellan Strait, then to sail northwards to 30°S, and finally to return home the same way. Although the name of the coastline in question has been obliterated, it has been convincingly argued, by K. R. Andrews, that the instruction to sail northwards cannot possibly refer to the legendary *Terra Australis* (an alternative hypothesis) which was

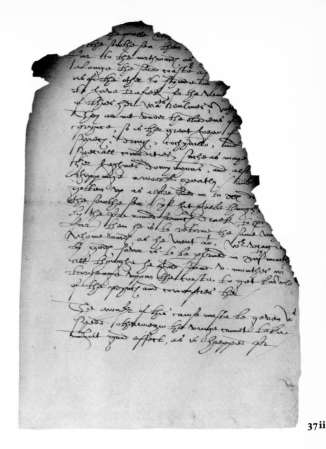

37 ii

supposed to stretch from the south of the Magellan Strait to the west as far as the East Indies. He further argues that the area of South America in question below 30°S was not in effective Spanish occupation, and might prove useful for trade or settlement. The proposal, as presented to Elizabeth in this document, had the merit of appearing law-abiding while leaving sufficient leeway for Drake to ensure the voyage was a financial success; an important, if not overriding, consideration for the promoters.

V

Crossing the Atlantic

ACRIMONY and mishap marred the fleet's progress to the coast of Brazil. There worsening weather, sickness and discontent amongst the crews finally culminated in Thomas Doughty's trial and execution. Although in contemporary accounts of the voyage a number of the gentlemen, ships' masters and crew members are mentioned, little is known about even the more prominent persons in Drake's complement. Ten gentlemen (sometimes twelve are recorded) ventured themselves, and presumably their money, on the voyage. Some were a constant source of discord on board. In command was Drake, usually titled 'the General', but sailing as his deputies were John Wynter, captain of the *Elizabeth*, and Thomas Doughty, evidently in charge of the military training of the men and later sent to command the *Pelican*. John Cooke, who recorded his account of the voyage for the annalist John Stow, described Wynter, Drake and Thomas Doughty 'as eqwall companyons and frindly gentlemen' in the voyage and this apparent division of responsibility was to have serious consequences as the voyage progressed.

Also on the voyage were Doughty's brother John, and George Fortescue, who wrote an account of the voyage now lost. Others included John Chester, commander of the *Swan*, Gregory Cary, Gregory Raymond, Emmanuel Watkins and a lawyer friend of Thomas Doughty, Leonard Vicary. Two other members of the company who may have been numbered amongst the gentlemen were John Audley and John Saracold. Saracold may be identifiable as John Saracold, Citizen and Draper of London. Both returned to England in the *Elizabeth*. Lawrence Eliot, otherwise unrecorded, was evidently a botanist of sorts, for he contributed to the collection of descriptions of plants observed on the voyage, which was published by Charles de l'Écluse at Antwerp in 1582. The company's chaplain was Francis Fletcher, whose illustrated journal of the voyage is now known through a late seventeenth century manuscript copy, and a much altered printed version, published by the compiler of *The World Encompassed* in 1628.

Of the ships' crews the most notable seamen were Drake's brother Thomas, John Drake, possibly a cousin who served as a page to Drake, and William Hawkins, nephew to John Hawkins. John Brewer the trumpeter, Thomas Blacoller, boatswain on the *Pelican* and Thomas Hood, who became master of the *Pelican* after Mr Cuttill's disgrace at Port Desire, are also mentioned in the texts from time to time.

All but the 'authorized' version printed in *The World Encompassed* 1628 relate the accumulation of dissension between Thomas Doughty and Drake on the voyage to the Straits.

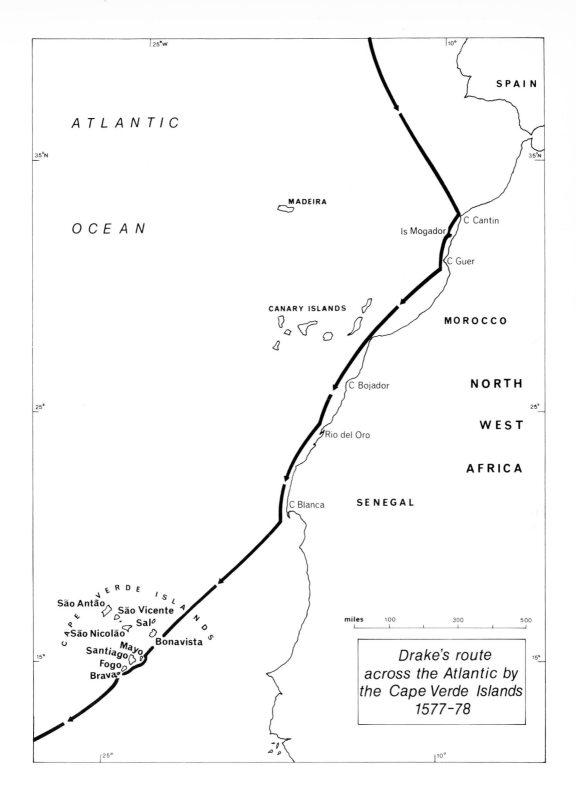

SPAIN

ATLANTIC

OCEAN

35°N   35°N

MADEIRA

C Cantin
Is Mogador
C Guer

CANARY ISLANDS

MOROCCO

NORTH

C Bojador

25°   25°

WEST

Rio del Oro

AFRICA

C Blanca   SENEGAL

miles   100   300   500

C   V E R D E   I S L A N D S
A
P   São Vicente
E   São Antão   Sal
São Nicolão
Mayo   Bonavista
Santiago
15°   Fogo   15°
Brava

*Drake's route
across the Atlantic by
the Cape Verde Islands
1577-78*

25°W

10°

25°

10°

In this expurgated and laudatory work dedicated by Drake's nephew, Sir Francis Drake, to Robert Dudley, Earl of Warwick, the compiler sought to exculpate Drake for his action against Doughty by referring to the great mischief 'which else had extended itselfe . . . to the violent shedding of innocent blood by murthering [murdering] our generall'. It may be inferred, however, from the evidence of Cooke's account and from the notes collected about the affair, presumably by John Stow, that Drake's main charge against Doughty was that he had sought to incite mutiny and, in all probability, to divert the voyage from its intended destination, the Pacific Ocean. When Doughty was brought to trial at Port St Julian a number of other crimes were alleged against him. These included *lèse majesté* (on the evidence of one Ned Bright, who claimed Doughty had said that the Queen and Privy Council could be corrupted by bribes), the charge of betraying the plans to Burghley, and of witchcraft. By the time the fleet reached Port Desire Drake had evidently decided to deal finally with Doughty. He went on board the *Elizabeth* and addressed the crew saying that 'he sent thythar a very bad couple of menn, the whiche he dyd not know how to cary along with hym this voyadge . . . [They were] Thomas Doughty who is a coniuer [*i.e.* conjurer], a sedytous fellow . . . and his brother the yonge Doughty, a wyche [*i.e.*witch], a poysonar.' In common with most men of the period Drake believed in the practical power of the Devil and his minions. In 1597 James VI of Scotland published a learned treatise on the nature of witchcraft and how to overcome it, entitled *Daemonologie*. Doughty moreover had the dubious talent of being able to read and write Greek and Hebrew, while his brother John was implicated in the rumour, then rife, that the Earl of Essex (Doughty's and Drake's late employer) had been poisoned. Whatever the cause of Drake's suspicions they soon hardened into an absolute conviction of his guilt. The thick coastal fogs prevailing along the inhospitable unknown coast of Patagonia fearfully named *Terra Demonum*, the presence of the 'giants' and their fires, and the prospect of the awesome Strait of Magellan all lent credence to the idea of Doughty's malicious power. For the voyage to succeed Doughty's removal was necessary. In the event his execution was the only satisfactory means of achieving this.

38 Drake's second-in-command

John Wynter's report of his voyage to the Strait of
Magellan under the command of Francis Drake,
dated 2 June 1579.
Endorsed: 'Voyadge of Mr. [   ] Wynter with
Mr. Drake to ye strayt of Magallanas June 1579.'
21 cm   *Lansdowne MS 100, no. 2*

'At the first when I cam from London [to
Plymouth] in greate hast wth one/shippe and
furniture in the same, answerable to the greatnes/
and lengthe of suche a viadge, thinkinge to have
found all/things readie I found contrarie to my
expectacon all things/unredie, for the shipps weare
moste untakled, most unbalested and unvictualled.'

On 19 September 1577, John Wynter, captain of the
Elizabeth, a ship of eighty tons and sixteen guns, set sail
from the port of London, in company with the *Benedict*,
a pinnace, in the charge of Thomas Moone, to join
Drake at Plymouth. Moone is generally considered to be
identifiable with the ship's carpenter who, on Drake's
orders, had secretly scuttled the *Swan* off Cartagena in
1572. Of John Wynter little is recorded. He was the son
of George Wynter, Clerk to the Navy, who purchased
the manor of Dyrham Park in 1571, and a nephew to Sir
William Wynter, Surveyor of the Queen's ships. Both
were backers of the intended voyage. John Wynter was a
friend of the lawyer, Thomas Doughty, who apparently
knew his uncle Sir William well. In an effort to save
Doughty from execution at Port St Julian, Wynter
offered to keep him safe on board the *Elizabeth*, but to no
avail.

Wynter furnished this somewhat critical report on his
return to England from the Strait of Magellan on 2 June
1579. Having failed to rendezvous with the *Golden Hind*,
Wynter claimed that his crew had refused to go for the
Moluccas. His declaration did not save him, however,
from the later accusation of desertion nor from
proceedings in the High Court of Admiralty in respect of
piracy (see below p. 98).

39 Sir Francis Drake (1540?–1596)

An engraved portrait of Francis Drake inscribed
'Franciscus Draco nobilissimus Angliae eques, rei
nauticae ac bellicae peritissimus 1598. Audentes
fortuna iuvat.' Signed 'C.V.P.' [*i.e.* Crispin van de
Passe.]   *see Frontispiece*
In: *Effigies regum ac principum*. [Cologne, 1598.]
14 cm   *812.l.2.(2)*

At five o'clock in the afternoon of 15 November 1577
Drake's fleet of five vessels set sail from Plymouth. The
ships were the *Pelican* of one hundred tons and eighteen
guns, commanded by Francis Drake, the ship's master
being Thomas Cuttill; the *Marigold*, a bark of thirty
tons and sixteen guns, with John Thomas as captain and
Nicholas Anthony as master; and the *Swan*, a fly-boat or
store-ship of fifty tons, in the charge of John Chester.
Together with the *Elizabeth* and the *Benedict* (see above)
the strength of the crews was recorded as '164 able and
sufficient men'. Also carried on board were four
pinnaces 'ready framed, but carried aboard in pieces' to
be built when the occasion arose.

By 16 November the ships had reached the Lizard but
were then forced by strong south-westerly winds to put
into Falmouth, where they were trapped by a storm for
about a week. 'Though it were in a very good harbor, yet
2 of our ships, viz., the admirall [*i.e.* the *Pelican*] . . . and
the *Marigold* were faine to cut their main masts by [*i.e.*
over] board.' In such a sorry state the fleet returned to
Plymouth where repairs were completed and the fleet set
sail for a second time on 13 December 1577.

One of eighteen historical portraits engraved by
Crispin van de Passe for this collection, the engraving
shows the circumnavigator aged about forty-three years.
The portrait is a close copy of the engraving made about
1590 by the Flemish artist, Jodocus Hondius, who was
then in London. At that time he was almost certainly
engaged on the design of a world map showing the
voyages of both Drake and Thomas Cavendish with
accompanying portraits set into the margin (see **78**).

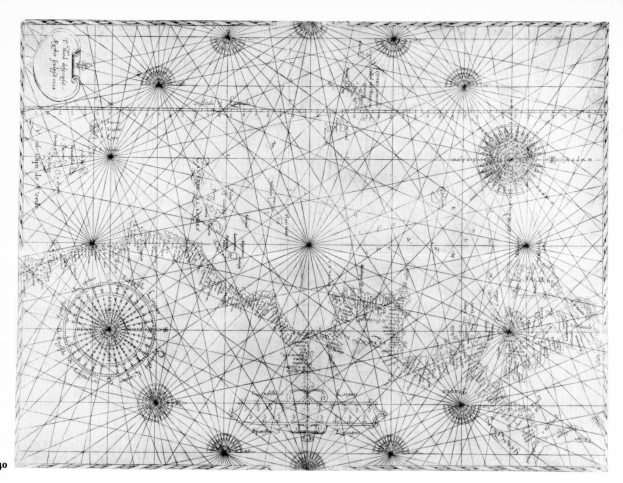

40 To the Cape Verde Islands

[A chart of the north east Atlantic showing the coasts of western Europe and north-west Africa from the British Isles to the Cape Verde islands.] T. Hood descripsit. A. Ryther, sculpsit 1592. 53 × 39 cm *Maps C.20.b.2.(2)*

So secret was the intended destination of the voyage that, apart from those privy to the promoters' plans, the fleet remained in ignorance until it was well out of sight of land. Drake then appointed the island of Mogadore off the coast of Morocco as a rendezvous, thus giving the first indication that the ships were not bound for Alexandria and the Levant trade. The master of the *Elizabeth*, William Markham, was later to complain that 'Mr. Drake hired him for Alexandria, but had he known that this [*i.e.* the Strait of Magellan] had been the Alexandria, he would have been hanged in England rather than have come on this voyage.'

The first land the *Pelican* sighted was Cape Cantine in Morocco, and on 27 December the fleet anchored at the north end of the island of Mogadore. A party of Moors were invited aboard where, despite religious pro-hibition, they drank wine 'abundantly'. Offers of mutual trade were made, but thwarted by the kidnapping of one of the shore party, John Fry, who was taken to the Sultan of Fesse to give an account of the voyage. He reported that the ships were bound for the Strait of Magellan. Before he could return, the fleet set sail for Cape Blanco *en route* for the Cape Verde islands. Fry eventually returned to England in a merchant ship.

This engraved chart of the north-east Atlantic, drawn by the mathematician and hydrographer Thomas Hood (fl. 1577–1604), was designed for the instruction of sailors in the art of navigation by use of the 'plane' chart.

The earliest 'educational' chart to be published in England, it was printed to accompany Hood's *The Mariner's Guide* which was published in his revision of William Bourne's *Regiment for the Sea*, 1596. The text makes clear that the chart was devised to illustrate, step-by-step, how to 'lay off' a course with a ruler and a pair of compasses or dividers; the standard equipment of the ship's master. A scale of latitude is added to the chart, by which the navigator could plot his observed position by cross-staff or astrolabe. A compass rose indicates the thirty-two points of the compass by which the course was set.

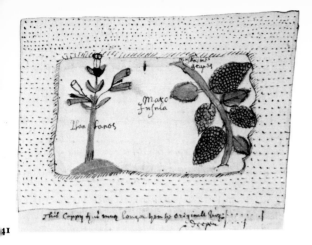

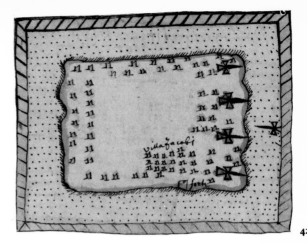

41 The Cape Verde Islands

An illustration of the island of Mayo in the Cape
Verde Islands, showing plantanes [*i.e.* bananas]
and muscadine grapes growing.
From a manuscript copy of Francis Fletcher's
account of the voyage written *ca* 1677, f. 6v.
14 × 16 cm   *Sloane MS 61*

Coasting down the west coast of North Africa, the fleet
reached Cape Blanco on 17 January. On the way three
canters or Spanish fishing vessels and three Portuguese
caravelles were captured. At the Cape, Thomas
Doughty trained his men 'in warlike order, for that they
myght not be unskilful in the time of need'. On 22
January the fleet departed for the island of Mayo in the
Cape Verde islands, to which the pilot of one of the
caravelles was obliged to guide them. He advised that
good supplies of *caberytas* or goat meat could be
obtained there. Winter and Doughty went ashore with
seventy men but failed to secure any provisions.

The island, as described by the chaplain, Francis
Fletcher, was verdant. Apart from the muscadine vines,
there grew two sorts of rare fruits, 'the one named *cocos*
[*i.e.* coconuts] which is the same as we call *nux Indica*,
and the other *plantanes* [*i.e.* bananas]'. This manuscript
account by Fletcher is now only known from a later copy
of the first part of the journal made by a John Conyers,
Citizen and Apothecary of London, about the year 1677
(Sloane MS 61). Conyers evidently also copied the set of
illustrations he found in the manuscript, for a caption
beneath the picture of 'Mayo Insula' reads: 'This Coppy
is much longer than the Originalle viz., deeper.'
Fletcher's manuscript was written some time after the
return of Thomas Cavendish in 1588 (to whom he
alludes) and before 1628 when *The World Encompassed*
was published, and which was based in part on
Fletcher's account (see **70**).

42 The capture of Nuño da Silva

An illustration of the island of Santiago in the
Cape Verde Islands, showing the town of S.
Jacobi (*i.e.* St James), and the Spanish fort.
From a manuscript copy of Francis Fletcher's
account of the voyage written *ca* 1677, f. 8.
14 × 16 cm   *Sloane MS 61*

The fleet left Mayo for the island of Santiago, ten
leagues to the west, on 31 January and coasted along the
southern end of the island still hoping for supplies. Two
Portuguese ships bound for Brazil were sighted and the
flagship gave chase. On board one of the ships was the
pilot and captain, Nuño da Silva, who later recorded his
capture for the Mexican Inquisition in May 1578. He
declared that he was a native of Oporto and had set sail
for Las Palmas to load 150 casks of wine for a trading
voyage to Brazil. He was about to cast anchor at Santiago
when he was captured by a fleet of six English ships. He
was at that time about sixty years old, of swarthy
complexion with a long beard and was, he thought, kept
on board the *Pelican* because he was known to be 'a pilot
for the coast of Brasilia, [and] that he might bring them
to such places in those contrys as had fresh water'. The
'authorized' account given in *The World Encompassed*
makes no mention of Nuño da Silva nor of the prize
taken, presumably because of the later court case in
which the Portuguese sued for restitution (see **98**).
Fletcher, however, described the vessel as laden 'with
singular wines, sackes and canaries [*i.e.* special types of
wine] with wollens and linens, silkes and velvetts'. She
was, he asserted, 'the life of our voyage, the neck
whereof otherwise had been broken for the shortness of
our provisions'.

The fleet, with Doughty in charge of the prize, passed
by the volcanic island of Fogo and took water on board at
Brava before setting da Silva's crew free in a pinnace
which had been reconstructed at Mogadore. Seven ships
(da Silva's included) then set sail for Brazil.

The caption to the drawing reads 'veria copia J.
Conyers'.

43 The Atlantic Ocean

A chart of the Atlantic showing the coasts of West Africa, Central and South America from 60°N to 44°S. Signed: 'Cyprian Sanchez A fez Em Lixª/dezembro 1596'.
MS coloured on vellum.
78 × 97 cm.   *Cotton MS Roll XIII.46*

It was Drake's sensible practice to take what navigational aids he could find on board captured vessels. On 23 May 1579 Nuño da Silva, on trial for heresy in Mexico, declared that Drake had taken from him 'my astrolabe, my navigation chart, which embraced however, only the Atlantic Ocean as far as the Rio de la Plata on the West and the Cape of Good Hope on the east, my book of instructions [*i.e.* rutter]'. On this chart of 1596 the coast to the Rio de la Plata is clearly shown and the principal coastal features to 44° south. It was drawn by Cyprian Sanchez, 'a master of navigation charts' to the Cosmographer Major of the Indies, and is thought to have been formerly in the collection of the Portuguese cartographer and historian, Joao Baptista Lavanha (*d.* 1624).

From the island of Santiago the fleet took a course south-southeast and crossed the Equator about 20 February. The ships experienced the usual calms, and heat which was such that the crews 'did sweate for the most part continually, as though wee had bene in a stove, or hote-house'. Fletcher and the other diarists also recorded the shoals of flying fish, dolphins and *bonitos* which replenished in some measure the ships' supplies. Nuño da Silva noted that the fleet was near the island of Fernando de Naronha (3°50′S), off the coast of Brazil, at the end of February, but the other accounts, notably those of Fletcher and Edward Cliffe, mariner, recorded that they fell in with the coast of Brazil on 5 April. On 10 March da Silva wrote hopefully but mistakenly that they were in a bay in 13°S and that Drake sailed for '*Spirito Santo* to put me on land and give me my ship'.

44 A rutter for the South Sea

'The heaighthes frome Cape Sant Vinsente southwarde.'
An English translation of a Portuguese rutter for the Atlantic Ocean and the Coast of South America, *ca* 1577, ff. 56v and 57.
28 cm   *Harley MS 167*

This translation from the Portuguese of a rutter or sailing directions from Cape St Vincent in the extreme south-west of Portugal to South America is included in a collection of sailing directions, compiled from both English and Portuguese sources. The directions give instructions for sailing in English and European waters as well as the rudiments of navigation and are accompanied by a 'Rutter to knowe youer Prime, and

your Epacke [*i.e.* Epact] whereby you may know the age of your mone [*i.e.* moon], necessary information for calculating the state of the tides in north west European ports. The table is set for the year 1578 and it therefore seems probable that the collection was compiled about that date if not a little before. Some such guide may well have been acquired by Drake from Nuño da Silva (see **43**).

The rutter gives the distances in Portuguese leagues (4 English miles) from place to place on the Brazilian coast, latitudes as far south as Magellan's Strait and the respective courses to be followed. Of particular interest is the section describing the Strait itself which gives the latitude of the eastern mouth of the Strait as 52°S. The course to be followed on leaving the Strait for the coast of Chile as far as *Serra Alta* (48°30′S) is north west, thus indicating the apparently universal misconception of mariners and chart-makers that the Pacific coastline of South America trended north west rather than northwards.

45 Thomas Doughty's speech on board the 'Pelican'

'The sum̃e of Thomas Doughtie his oration upon the pellica[n]/when he came from [the] price [*i.e.* prize] to the pellican/to Remayne the companie being called by the Botteswain together.'
In a collection of manuscripts entitled 'Sr Fraunsis Drake's voyage wᵗʰ his proseeding againste Thomas Doughtye.' f. 7.
33 cm   *Harley MS 6221*

Described by Fletcher as a paragon of virtue and learning, Thomas Doughty was a well-educated gentleman and a lawyer. From his will it is evident that he was an adventurer in the voyage for a sum of not more than £500, although his name does not appear in the memorandum drawn up for the voyage in 1577 (see **37**). He had earlier served as a soldier and secretary to the Earl of Essex in Ireland where he had met Drake and was later private secretary to Christopher Hatton. He insisted, according to hostile witnesses, that he had been instrumental in Drake's preferment and had introduced Drake to Walsingham and the Privy Council to promote the voyage. Whether this was more boast than fact, he was probably privy to the promoters' plans and was evidently highly regarded and trusted by Drake, at least until he took command of the Portuguese prize taken at Santiago. The first sign of conflict arose almost immediately over the ship's goods. Doughty and Drake's brother Thomas (whom Cooke described as 'not the wisest of men in Christendom'), accused each other of pilfering. Drake soon heard of the quarrel. On finding Doughty in possession of 'some pares of Portugall gloves, some few peces of money . . . and a small ring' (which Doughty claimed had been given him in the hope of favours by the prisoners), he accused

43 Fish and birds seen in the Atlantic (*Sloane MS 61 f. 13*).

Doughty of seeking to discredit him by unjustly accusing his brother, Thomas Drake. In spite of the violent quarrel, Doughty was then sent to take charge of the *Pelican* while Drake kept control of the valuable prize.

On taking command, Doughty gathered the company together and exhorted them to obey the ship's master Mr Cuttill in matters of navigation, and himself, as Drake's deputy, in all other cases. In view of later events it is perhaps significant that he claimed 'the Generall [*i.e.* Drake] hath his authority from the Queen's majesty . . . to punish at his discretion with death or other ways offenders; so he hath committed the same authority to me in his absence . . .'. The long voyage to Brazil seems to have lent itself to indiscreet talk between Doughty and Mr Cuttill (who was later disgraced). Cuttill was said to have been bribed by Doughty 'to gooe to the sea withe [*sic*], and doe thear what he thought meete to make retorne off their money wth advantage' (Harley MS 6221 f. 8). Doughty had evidently suggested that the *Pelican* should make its own independent raid on Spanish and Portuguese shipping to ensure a good financial return on his and the other gentlemen's investments. Certainly much later in the voyage Drake offered this as the reason for Doughty's execution to a Spanish prisoner, Francisco de Zarate.

46 The execution of Thomas Doughty

John Cooke's account of the voyage from
Plymouth to the Strait of Magellan. ff. 93–110.
MS 24 cm   *Harley MS 540.*

John Cooke sailed aboard the prize, renamed the *Mary*, and recorded his account of the voyage, with particular reference to Doughty's beheading, for the annalist, John Stow. An ardent supporter of Doughty, he disliked Drake intensely and complained bitterly that Drake had forced him to sleep in the open at Port St Julian dressed only in doublet and hose. Much of what he recorded is, however, corroborated in part by the other accounts and his story of the events leading to Doughty's execution is much the most convincing.

On 5 April the *Mary* fell in with the coast of Brazil and John Brewer, the trumpeter who had been recommended to Drake by Hatton, was sent across to the *Pelican*. There, he claimed, Doughty saw fit to hit him and he, in turn, called Doughty no friend to Drake, which was tantamount to an accusation of mutiny. Cooke heard the tale from Brewer himself on his return to the prize, and shortly afterwards Doughty was sent without a hearing to the *Swan* under the command of Mr Chester. At this point hampered by coastal fogs and storms as the fleet sailed south, Drake became convinced that Doughty was not only mutinous but also conjuring up the foul weather. He was no doubt encouraged in his views by the ships' crews, whose animosity towards Doughty and some of the other gentlemen was evident. The master of the flyboat sat to his meals with the crew rather than with Doughty, Chester and the other gentlemen on board. For lack of a fit crew the *Swan* was burned at Port Desire (47°45′S) and Doughty, now fearing for his life, was transferred to the Spanish *canter*. When that too was given up, Drake placed Doughty and his brother John in the *Elizabeth* under John Wynter's charge, warning them not to read or write except in English for fear of their conjuring. At Port St Julian, which they reached on 20 June 1578, Doughty was tried before a jury of twelve men with John Wynter as foreman on a number of charges summed up by Drake as follows: 'You have heare sought by dyvers means, in as myche as you maye, to discredite me, to the greate hindrance and ovarthrowe of this voyage, besydes other greate mattars . . .'. In the event it seems that Drake was finally incensed by Doughty's own admission that he had given Burghley 'a plott of the voyadge'. Burghley had evidently been excluded from the plans for the voyage and indeed he remained opposed to the voyage even after Drake's lucrative return. The jury found Doughty guilty and on a show of hands by the ships' company he was sentenced to death. As was customary Doughty made a dignified and forgiving end, praying for Her Majesty the Queen, and for the success of the voyage. He then asked to be remembered to his friends, especially Sir William Wynter, before 'imbrasynge the Generall, [and] namynge hym his good Capitayne'. He was beheaded on 2 July 1578.

47 Thomas Doughty's Will

Will signed by Thomas Doughty 11 September 1577 and proved 15 October 1579 together with a codicil.
MS 45 cm   *P.R.O. PROB. 11/61/40 f. 313d*

In June 1579 news of Doughty's death reached England. On 15 October 1579, almost a year before Drake's own return, Doughty's will was proved. To it Doughty had added a codicil. Presumably he did this at Port St Julian when he realized that he was to be beheaded and buried overseas. Instead of allowing for funeral expenses, which he would be needing no longer, he distributed the amount amongst his friends. The principal beneficiary was Leonard Vicary, gentleman, of the Inner Temple, his close companion on the voyage, who received £40, 'in consideration of his faithfull and true friendship and great travaile by him sustained in this voyag'. Vicary, alone, is recorded as having questioned the legality of Doughty's trial and, for his pains, was dubbed a 'crafty lawyer' by Francis Drake.

VI

The Strait of Magellan, gateway to the South Seas

I N 1577 the Strait of Magellan was still the only known western passage from the Atlantic Ocean round the continent of America into the Pacific. First discovered by Ferdinand Magellan in 1520, it had become a place of ill omen on account of the danger of its navigation and the failures of later expeditions. By the middle of the sixteenth century, as James Burney recorded in *A Chronological History of the Discoveries in the South Sea*, vol. 1 (1803), p. 245, there was a saying that the passage had closed up and a superstition that 'all who were principally concerned in the discovery of the South Sea, had come to an untimely end: Basco Nuñez de Balboa was beheaded; Magalhanes was killed by infidels; Ruy Falero died raving; the Mariner De Lepe, who first discovered the Strait from the topmast, turned renegado, and became a Mahometan.' Lopez Vaz observed, in Hakluyt's words: 'The seeking of these Streights of Magellan is so dangerous, and the voyage so troublesome, that it seemeth a matter almost impossible to be perfourmed, insomuch that for the space of thirty yeeres no man made account thereof; untill of late one Francis Drake.'

Once the Spaniards had established their regular trade routes between Mexico and Manila, and between Peru, Panama and Mexico, they had reason to keep their charts and rutters out of foreign hands in the hope that ignorance of the navigation would deter intruders. They were also accused of spreading false rumours. One of these was the report that the Strait was not repassable, that a strong current, driven by easterly winds, set westward through the strait and made it impossible for a ship to return. With the prevailing westerlies the coast of Chile was a lee shore, 'not to be enterprised without great peril'; and the instructions to the Spanish navigator Pedro Sarmiento de Gamboa in 1579 show that the Spaniards themselves believed the western entrance almost impossible to find, 'owing to the innumerable openings and channels which there are before arriving at it, where many discoverers have been lost.' Sent to dispel the Spaniards' 'dread of the navigation' by surveying the Strait, Sarmiento was the first to find and enter the western mouth on a voyage from Chile.

For his achievement as the first Englishman to navigate the Strait and enter the Pacific Ocean, Drake won great popular acclaim. 'Such a mighty and valuable thing also was the passing this Straight, that Sir Francis Drake's going thro' it, gave birth to that famous Old Wives Saying, *viz.* that Sir Francis Drake shot the Gulph; a Saying that was current in England for many Years, I believe near a Hundred after Sir Francis Drake was gone his long Journey of all; as if

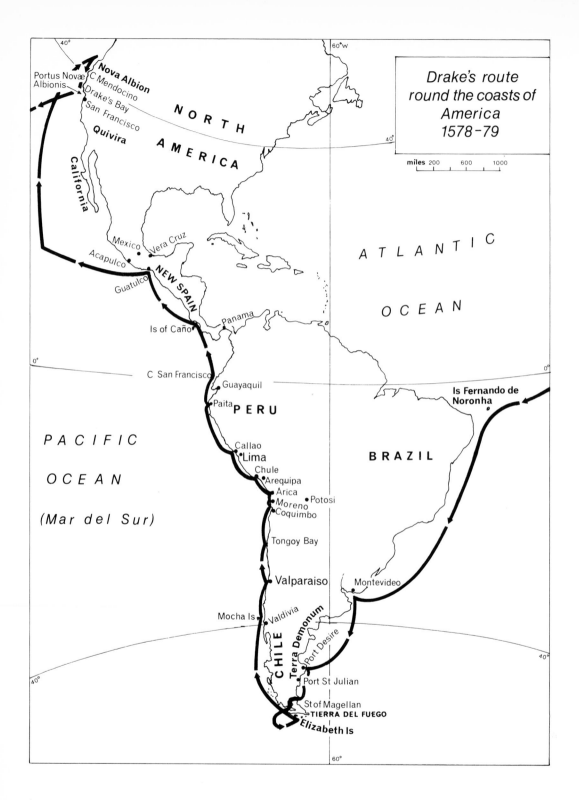

Drake's route
round the coasts of
America
1578-79

miles 200   600   1000

40°

NORTH

AMERICA

Nova Albion
Portus Novæ
Albionis
C Mendocino
Drake's Bay
San Francisco
Quivira

California

Mexico   Vera Cruz
Acapulco
Guatulco
NEW SPAIN

Is of Caño
Panama

ATLANTIC

OCEAN

40°

0°   0°

C San Francisco
Guayaquil
Paita   PERU

PACIFIC

OCEAN

(Mar del Sur)

Callao
Lima
Chule
Arequipa
Arica
Moreno   Potosi
Coquimbo

Tongoy Bay

Valparaiso

Mocha Is   Valdivia

CHILE

Terra Demonum

Port Desire

Is Fernando de
Noronha

BRAZIL

Montevideo

40°

Port St Julian

St of Magellan
TIERRA DEL FUEGO
Elizabeth Is

60°W   60°

there had been but one Gulph in the world, and that passing it had been a wonder next to that of Hercules cleansing the Egean Stable.' Thus Daniel Defoe's imaginary circumnavigator commented in *A New Voyage round the World, by a Course Never Sailed Before* (1725).

Drake's successful navigation not only disproved the reported adverse currents, but also provided the first indications that the Strait did not divide America from a southern continent, that it was not the only route between the Atlantic and the Pacific Oceans. On entering the South Sea and standing north-westward, Drake's fleet was beset by storms and scattered never to meet again. Drake thereupon sailed the *Pelican*, now renamed the *Golden Hind*, on a southerly course which in about 55°S revealed Tierra del Fuego to be an archipelago with open sea beyond. 'Their is neither Continent current nor Streight', Fletcher wrote, arguing that a strait was only properly so-called if it divided two continents. The prohibition on publication prevented Drake from gaining proper credit for this discovery. It was proclaimed in retrospect, when news reached England in 1617 that the Dutchmen Jacob Le Maire and Willem Schouten had discovered in 1616 the route by way of Le Maire Strait round Cape Horn. Drake was then said to have discovered many years before that Tierra del Fuego was an archipelago and even to have seen Cape Horn itself. The maps of the late 1580s and 1590s depicting the archipelago of the 'Elizabethides' to the south of the American continent show that Drake had revealed the probability of the new route. This route was in due course to supersede the passage through the Strait as the gateway to the Pacific. Thus in 1728 Defoe was to describe the Strait as 'a Place, which may perhaps be as entirely forgotten in the World, as if it had never been known'.

That the saying 'Drake shot the Gulf' remained for so many years current parlance, with legends woven around it, indicates the historic import of Drake's exploits in the eyes of his fellow-countrymen. At a time when the strictest secrecy concealed the details of the voyage, the event of his 'shooting the gulf' could be fearlessly acclaimed, conveying the main fact of the voyage: that Drake had broken into the forbidden world of the South Seas, round which lay the richest empires in the world.

48 Drake harangues the company

John Cooke's account.
24 cm   *Harley MS 540. ff. 107ᵛ–108ʳ*

'Nay, softe, Mastar Fletcher (qd. he) I must preache this daye my selfe.' With these words Drake on 11 August 1578 began his long speech to the whole company assembled in a tent on shore at Port St Julian. Immediately after Doughty's execution, Drake had ordered the company to receive Communion on the following Sunday, 5 July, so that all old quarrels might be forgiven. As further days of winter passed, privation, sickness and dissension increased. Drake now admonished the gentlemen and the sailors to put aside their differences: 'we are very far from owr contry and frinds, we are compassed in on every syde with owr enemyes . . . Wherefore we muste have these mutines and discords that are growne amongest us redrest, for . . . here is suche controversye betwene the saylars and the gentlemen, and such stomakynge betwene the gentlemen and saylars, that it dothe even make me madd to here it . . . for I must have the gentleman to hayle and draw with the mariner, and the maryner with the gentleman . . .'. To his offer that any wishing to return home should take themselves off in the *Marigold*, none would (or dared) agree. Drake then expounded the purpose of the voyage, claiming the full support of the Queen. Summoned to interview with the Queen, he had represented his plan to her as a course of revenge against the King of Spain: 'thonly waye was to anoy hym by his Indyes'; the Queen had answered that if any one in her realm gave the King of Spain information, they should lose their heads. He ended his harangue with the words 'it is only hir maiestie that you serve and this voyadge is only her setting forthe'.

Cooke's account reads as reliable testimony of the proceedings, although he was a hostile witness. With this speech Drake braced his men for the next and more dangerous part of the navigation, the passage through the dreaded Strait of Magellan.

49 The route of Magellan's circumnavigation

Map of the world showing Magellan's route in an atlas of charts inscribed 'Baptista Agnesius Ianuensis fecit Venetijs 1536 die 13 October'.
41 × 58 cm   *Additional MS 19927, Map 13*

A Genoese who worked in Venice, the chart-maker Baptista Agnese was celebrated for his series of manuscript atlases drawn in portolan style, and produced from about 1535 until some time after 1556. Most of the atlases included an oval world map based originally on a Spanish model, such as that here exhibited, and depicting the track of Magellan's

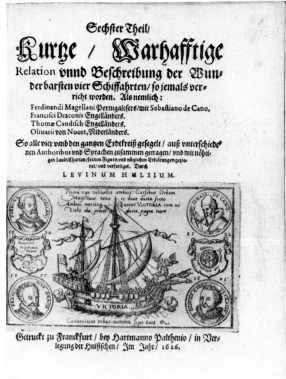

49

expedition westward to the Moluccas and round the world, 1519–22. Although bearing the date 1536 on the diagram of the zodiac, this atlas is more typical of the Agnese atlases made after 1545. An earlier version of about 1535, in which the oval world map does not display Magellan's track, belonged to Lord Lumley, and was in the Old Royal Library (*Old Royal MS 14.C.V.*). A stylized view of Magellan's ship the *Victoria* is shown on the title-page to Levinus Hulsius: *Sechster Theil. Kurze Warhafftige* (1626) here illustrated.

50 America the Fourth Part of the World

Americae Sive Quartae Orbis Partis. Nova et Exactissima Descriptio. Auctore Diego Gutiero Philippi Regis Hisp. etc. Cosmographo Hiero Cock Excuda, 1562.
93 × 94 cm   *Maps 69810. (18)*

Diego Gutierrez, Cosmographer to King Philip II of Spain, and acting Pilot Major, depicts on this map the Spanish empires in the New World *ca* 1550. The largest printed map of America to date, it was engraved by Hieronymous Cock in 1562, eight years after Diego Gutierrez's death. The Patagonian giants towering over a Spanish soldier in 'Tierra de Patagones', 'Gigantum Regio', and the southern continent 'Tierra de

Magellanes' in the far south, are typical features of South American geography. The map is believed to be the first printed map to use the name California, applied to the southern tip of Lower California ('C. California').

51   Survey of the Strait of Magellan

'The Land of Patagona &c. The Draught of Magellan Straits drawn by Captain Iohn Narbrough annᵒ 1670: on board his Maiestis shipp Sweepstaks as I pased and repased the Straits'.
MS coloured on vellum. 80 × 186 cm

K. Top. CXXIV. 84

Captain John Narborough was the first Englishman to sail through the Strait of Magellan to Chile and back. His expedition of 1669–70 was designed 'to make a Discovery both of the Seas and Coasts of that part of the World, and if possible to lay the foundation of a Trade there'. The results of the survey are recorded on this draught, comprising the earliest large-scale chart of the Strait. Features of topography and hydrography are displayed in detail, together with the customs and characteristics of the inhabitants (see **60**). First published in 1673, the derived engraved map remained for many years the standard guide for the navigation of the Strait.

51

52 Fletcher's duck – the penguin

*Historisch Ende Wijdtloopigh verhael, van t'ghene
de vijf Schepen (die int Jaer 1698 [sic] tot
Rotterdam toegherust zijn, om door de Straet
Magellana haren handel te dryven) wedervaren is,
tot den 7. September 1599, op welcken dagt
Capiteyn Sebald de Weerdt, met twee Schepen door
onweder vande Vlote versteken is . . .* door M.
Barent Iansz. Amstelredam, 1617.
20 cm   *983.ff. 6 (vol. 2)*

52i

'In these Ilands', Fletcher wrote, 'we found great reliefe
and Plenty of good victualls, for Infinite were the
numbers of the fowle, wch the welsh men named
Pengwin, and Maglanus tearmed them geese . . . It is not
Possible to find a bird, of their bignes, to have greater
strength than they, for our men putting in cudgells into
their earths to force them out they wold take hold of
them with their Bills & would not lett goe their hold
fast.'
   Fletcher's description of hunting the penguin (Sloane
MS 61. f. 29^v) is illustrated in the scene of Dutchmen in
the Strait of Magellan in January 1600. Barent Janssen
served as surgeon under Captain Sebald de Weerdt in
the fleet of the Admirals Jacques Mahu and Simon de
Cordes, which set out from Rotterdam in 1598 to sail for
the Far East via the Strait of Magellan. Fletcher's
drawings of a 'duck like fowl' and seal (f. 15) are
illustrated here.

52ii

53 The Spaniards fortify the Strait, 1584

Deliniatio Freti Magellanici
In: Levinus Hulsius: *Sechste Theil. Kurtze
Warhafftige Relation und beschreibung der
Winderbarsten vier Schiffarten so jemals verricht
worden.* Nuremberg, 1603.
16 × 12 cm   *C.114.c.20*

Spurred into urgent countermeasures by Drake's bold
incursion into the South Sea and his raids on Spanish
settlements, the Viceroy of Peru sent the navigator
Pedro Sarmiento de Gamboa on an expedition from
Peru to the Strait of Magellan in 1579–80 to intercept
Drake on his return, 'it being public fame that Francisco
would return by the Strait, as he now knew where it
was.' Sarmiento was also to make a survey of the strait to
discover the best way of closing it against intruders.
Proceeding to Spain with plans to fortify the Strait and
to settle a colony, Sarmiento was despatched by King
Philip in 1581 with a colonizing expedition and a great
fleet under the command of Don Diego Flores de
Valdes. 'These ships had the hardest hap of any that ever
went out of Spaine since the Indias were first
discovered', wrote Lopez Vaz. Of twenty-three galleons
and 3,500 soldiers, few ships or men returned. The

53

colonies of Nombre de Jesus and Don Felipe which Sarmiento settled on the shores of the strait in 1584 met with like disaster. Named on Hulsius's map 'Philippopolis', Don Felipe was a ruined deserted settlement when Thomas Cavendish visited it in 1587 and renamed the place Port Famine.

54 The Pelican is re-named the Golden Hind

A model of an armed early Jacobean vessel.
Dimensions: height 50 cm; length 69 cm; width 18 cm *Lent by the Ashmolean Museum*

On 20 August 1578 the *Pelican* reached Cape Virgins at the entrance to the Strait. There, Drake, 'in remembrance of his honourable friend and favorer, Sir Christopher Hatton, changed the name of the shippe which himselfe went in from the *Pelican* to be called the *Golden Hind*'. One of the main backers of the voyage and a Royal favourite, Christopher Hatton was not only Drake's patron but also the employer of Thomas

Doughty. His crest a 'hind trippant or' was the inspiration for the new name which was presumably given to the ship to compliment Hatton and, as has been suggested, to allay any suspicions Hatton might entertain about Drake's motives in executing Doughty.

The ship model illustrates the shape of a late Elizabethan vessel or early Jacobean vessel, while the rigging is generally thought to be of the early Jacobean type. The model is roughly executed and is not to scale, although one inch is approximately equal to five feet. As such it was probably made by a sailor rather than by a master shipwright like Phineas Pett who has been suggested as the author of the model. It is unlikely to have been made to represent the *Golden Hind* and, as its provenance is unclear, the model may not even be of English origin. The ship is however one of the earliest known examples and was probably catalogued in the 1680s as one of two such ship models then in the Ashmolean Museum: 'Duae naves prostratae exactè structae, variisque tormentis bellicis ex ligno elaboratis exonoratae.' (*1685 Catalogue, B.758.*)

55 Wynter's bark

Caroli Clusii Atreb. aliqvot notæ in Garciæ
Aromatum Historiam. eiusdem descriptiones
nonnullarum Stirpium, & aliarum exoticarum
rerum, quæ à Generoso vir Francisco Drake . . .
obseruatæ sunt . . . Antverpiæ, 1582.
17 cm   *988.f.2.(2)*

In the storm which beset the ships as they sailed north-west from the Strait of Magellan Drake lost the *Marigold* on 28 September 1578 and then, on the night of 7 October, the *Elizabeth*. Returning into the Strait, the *Elizabeth* stayed for three weeks in a sound, 'The Port of Health', so named because Wynter took measures there to restore the health of his men. He collected the plant later named in his honour *Drimys winteri* by J. R. Forster and G. Forster, and used the bark with great success for treating several cases of scurvy. Wynter brought home specimens of the bark which he presented to the famous botanist Clusius (Charles de l'Écluse), who came to London in 1581 and met Wynter and Lawrence Eliot. In his handbook on aromatic plants Clusius here describes and illustrates the winter-bark (pp. 30–31), giving it the name *Winteranus Cortex*. The bark is aromatic and pungent, with tonic and antiscorbutic qualities.

Clusius's record of Drake's botanical discoveries is notable as giving the first published account of the voyage, Nicholas Breton's *Discourse* being more of a 'celebration' (**94**).

56 Peter Carder's strange adventures; and John Wynter's return

'The Relation of Peter Carder . . .' In: Samuel
Purchas *Purchas His Pilgrimes* Vol. 4 (1625),
pp. 1187–90.
34 cm   *679.h.14*

Shortly after the separation of the *Elizabeth*, as they lay off Tierra del Fuego, Drake put eight men in a small pinnace and ordered them to wait upon the ship 'for all necessary uses'. During the night in foul weather they lost the *Golden Hind*. Lacking provisions, maps and compass, they returned to the Strait where they were attacked and captured by Indians. Only Peter Carder survived. After some years with the Portuguese in Brazil, he was picked up by an English ship near the Azores, reaching England at the end of November 1586, nine years and fourteen days after his departure on the voyage. Carder reports that he was granted an audience with the Queen at Whitehall, 'where it pleased her to talke with me a long houres space of my travailes and wonderful escape, and among other things of the manner of M. Dowties execution; and afterward bestowed 22. angels on me . . .'. E. G. R. Taylor (1930) has suggested that the placing of Peter Carder and his mates in the pinnace might have been a further step to

eliminate dissidents, but there is no evidence for or against this explanation of the curious incident.

In the marginal note Purchas records his conference with Wynter at Bath in September 1618: 'which told me that solemne possession was actually taken of those parts, to the use of her Majesty . . .'. Wynter's decision to return home in November 1578 had been recorded by Edward Cliffe in Hakluyt's *Principal Navigations* III (1600), pp. 748–9: 'We came out of this harbour (the "Port of Health") the first of November, giving over our voiage by M. Winters compulsion (full sore against the mariners minds) who alledged, he stood in dispaire, as well to have winds to serve his turne for Peru, as also for M. Drakes safety.' Although contrary to Wynter's testimony (**38**), that 'the Master did utterly dislike of' the voyage, John Cooke provides independent corroborative evidence that Wynter himself decided to return: 'and then for owr returne I thinke owr Captayne, Master Wynter, wyll aunswer, who toke the peryll on hym.' (*Harley MS 540, f. 110ʳ*.)

58

57 The uttermost cape

Sketch map of the southern extremity of South
America by Francis Fletcher.
MS 23 × 16 cm   *Sloane MS 61.f. 35ʳ*

Blown south by the storm encountered on leaving the Strait of Magellan, Drake sought the shelter of a group of islands, the southernmost of which he named Elizabeth Island. On his sketch map Fletcher depicts the islands as an archipelago, challenging the contemporary theory that Tierra del Fuego was part of the southern

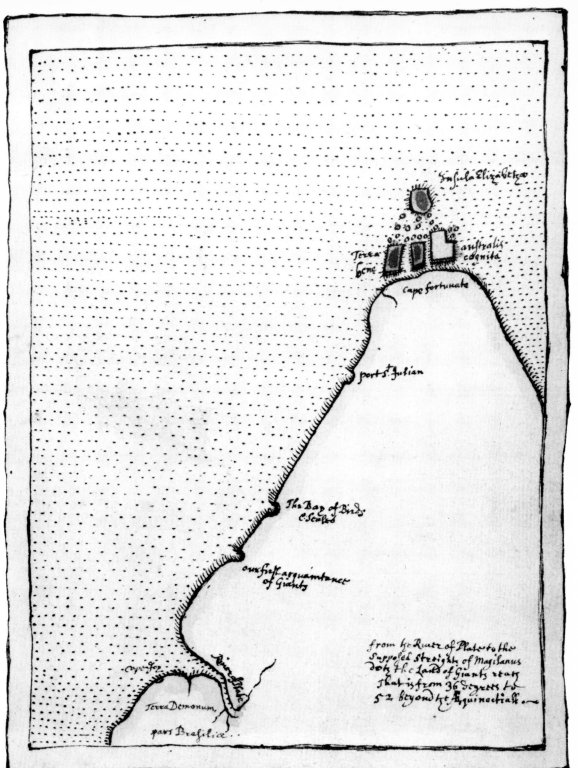

Insula Elizabethæ

Terra bona

australis cognita

Cape fortunate

port St Julian

The Bay of Birds
C. Scales

our first acquaintance
of Giants

from ye River of Plate to the
Supposed streight of Magilanus
doth the Land of Giants reach
That is from 36 degrets to
52 beyond ye Æquinoctiall

Cape Joy

Ryver of Plate

Terra Demonum

pars Brasiliæ

57

continent. 'Wee departing hence and takeing our farewell from the southernmost part of the world knowne, or as wee think to be knowne now, Wee altered the name of those Southerly Ilands from *terra incognita* . . . to terra nunc bene cognita,' Fletcher wrote in his journal (f. 37^v). 'The uttermost cape or hedland of all these Ilands, stands neere in 56 deg., without which there is no maine nor Iland to be seene to the Southwards, but that the Atlanticke Ocean and the South Sea, meete in a most large and free scope. It hath beene a dreame through many ages, that these Ilands have been a maine . . .' (*The World Encompassed* [1628]). Elizabeth Island is identified as Henderson Island, 55°36′S, 69°05′W, lying about 60 miles north-west of Cape Horn.

58   Fletcher's account of Elizabeth Island

'The first part of the second voiage about the world attempted continued and happily accomplished Within the tyme of 3 yeares by M^r ffrancis Drake, at her highness commaund & his company written & faithfully layed downe by ffrancis ffletcher minister of Christ, & Preacher of the Gospell adventurer & traueler in the same voyage.'
23 cm   *Sloane MS 61. ff. 38^v–39^r*

Fletcher's map of Elizabeth Island (Henderson Island, 55°36′S) illustrates Drake's most southerly discovery. Fletcher writes: 'My selfe being landed did with my boy travill to the southermost point of the Iland . . . where I found that Iland to be more Southerly three partes of a degree than anny of the rest of the Ilands. Where haveing sett up on end a Stone of som biggnes & with such tooles as I hadd of Purpose ever about mee when I went one shore, had engraven her Majestyes name, her Kingdom, the year of Christ and the day of the moneth, I returned againe in some Reasonable tyme to our company.'

This manuscript comprises a copy of the notes and drawings made by Francis Fletcher, a gentleman-volunteer who sailed as Chaplain. The copyist was John Conyers, 'Pharmacopolist' (see **41, 43**). Only the first part survives, covering the voyage as far as the Island of Mocha.

59   Drake embraces the southermost point of the World

The Observations of S^{ir} Richard Hawkins Knight, in his vojage into the South Sea. Anno Domini 1593.
24 cm   *566.g.23.(2)*

Describing his own voyage through the Strait of Magellan into the South Sea in 1593, the navigator Sir Richard Hawkins confirms the discovery (as revealed by the maps of Drake's voyage) that a sailor 'may keepe the mayne Sea, and goe round about the Straites to the Southward, and it is the shorter way'. He records Drake's report to him: 'I remember, that Sir Francis Drake told me, that having shott the Straites, a storme took him . . . and that at the end of the storme, he found himselfe in fiftie degrees, which was sufficient testimony and proofe, that he was beaten round about the Straites'.

Taken with Fletcher's journal (**58**), Drake's report to Hawkins suggests that Drake and Fletcher, with Fletcher's boy, went on shore at Elizabeth Island; and that Fletcher set up and carved the stone while Drake effected a curious act of possession: 'going a-shore, [he] carried a Compasse with him, and seeking out the Southermost part of the Iland, cast himselfe downe upon the uttermost poynt groveling, and so reached out his bodie over it. Presently he imbarked, and then recounted unto his people, that he had bene upon the Southermost knowne land in the world, and more further to the Southwards upon it, then any of them, yea, or any man as yet knowne.' The 'Mellon' map of Drake's voyage displays a flag on Elizabeth Island to record this act of possession (see **75**).

60   Artefacts of the Patagonian and Tierra del Fuegan Indians

a   Rattle made of raw-hide.
Possibly *Tehuelche*, Patagonia
Length approx. 34 cm
                   Lent by the Museum of Mankind, 2148

'The Giants Musicall instrument' drawn by Fletcher was a Patagonian rattle. Writing of the Indians at Port Desire, Fletcher records that they used rattles made of bark which they hung at their girdles when dancing. In later times a rattle of dried bladder or hide was used in music-making. According to the information given by the donor of this specimen (Lieut Thomas Graves, RN), the rattle was used by the natives to drive away evil spirits by the side of a sick person. It was made of a large bladder with pebbles in it.

b   Necklace made of shells strung on sinew.
Probably *Yahgan*, Tierra del Fuego.
Length (drop) approx. 39 cm
                   Lent by the Museum of Mankind, NN Holmested

c   Necklace of bone strung on sinew.
Yahgan, Tierra del Fuego.
Length (drop) approx. 33 cm
                   Lent by the Museum of Mankind, 1926–44.
                   (Presented by Rupert Vallentin, Esq.)

The *Yahgan* used two kinds of necklace. One was made of shells (usually *Photinula violacea*), which were perforated near the lip and strung with a spiral wrapping technique upon sinew. The sinew was sometimes

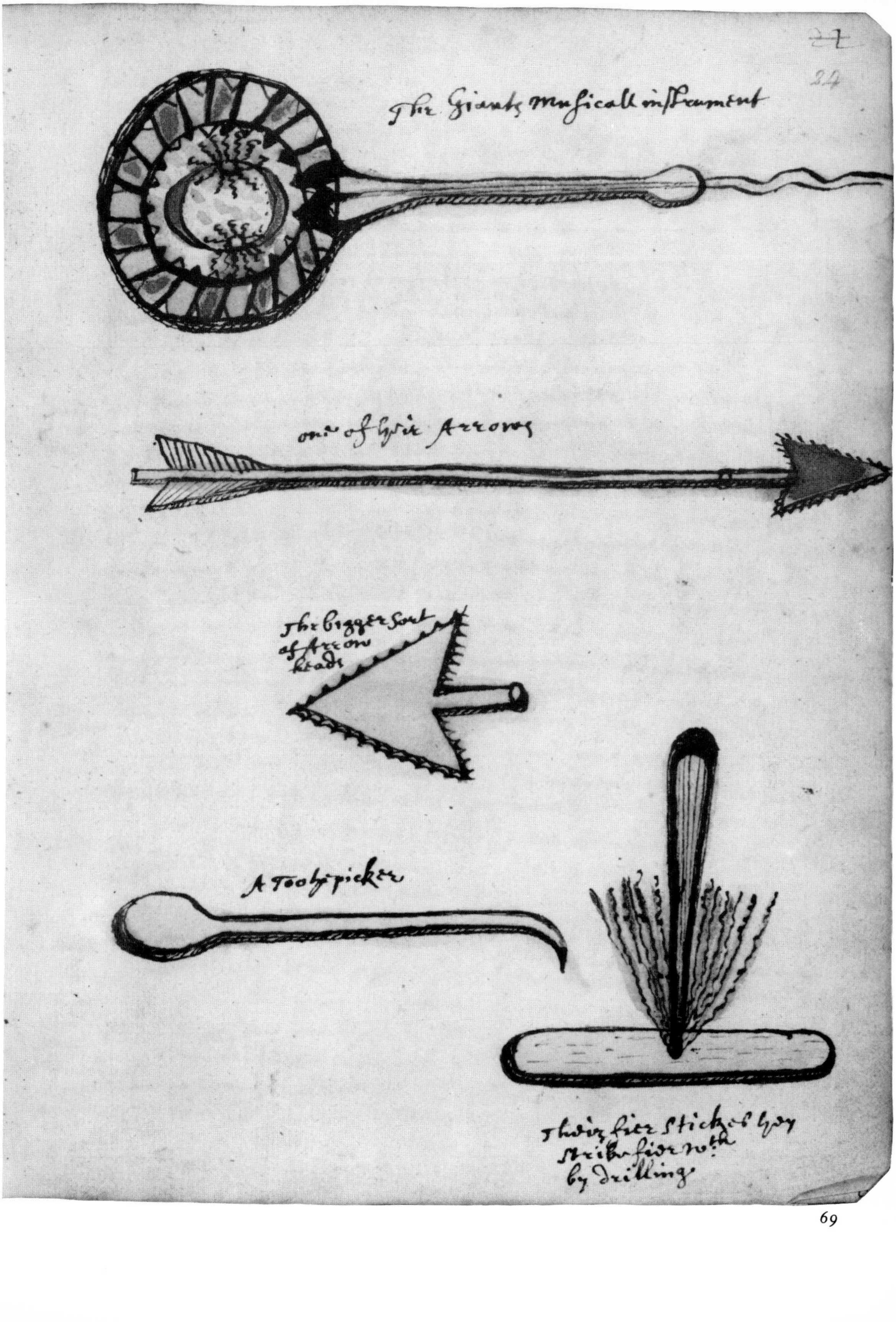

The Giants musicall instrument

one of their Arrows

The bigger sort
of Arrow
heads

A Toothpicker

their fier sticke they
strike fier with
by drilling

stained to a red colour. The other type was made from cylindrical sections of bone cut from leg bones of gulls or ducks strung upon sinew, which was sometimes braided. Patagonian women depicted on Narborough's chart (**51**) are wearing necklaces, which Narborough describes as made of 'small glistening shells'.

d Feather headdress.
Probably *Yahgan*.
Length approx. 77 cm
Lent by the Museum of Mankind, NN '97'

Robert Fitz-Roy (*Narrative of the surveying voyages of his Majesty's ships Adventure & Beagle . . . 1839*) records that 'A fillet is often worn around the head, which upon ordinary occasions is simply a string, made of sinews; but if going to war or dressed for show, the fillet is ornamented with white down, white feathers, or pieces of cloth, if they have obtained any from shipping. . . .' *Yahgan* shaman also had diadems of heron plumes and kelp-goose down, and white paint, as part of their ceremonial regalia. On his chart (**51**) Narborough shows various people in headdress.

e Bone spear head or harpoon dart head.
Length approx. 28 cm
Lent by the Museum of Mankind, 1921. 10–14, 82

Fletcher illustrates 'the bigger sort of arrow heads'.

f Bone spear head
Length 39 cm
Lent by the Museum of Mankind, 1919. 11–4, 35

g Bow
Length 120 cm
Lent by the Museum of Mankind, no. 287

Several of Narborough's Indians (**51**) hold bows and arrows of various kinds.

h Stone projectile points.
Lent by the Museum of Mankind

i Three arrows
Lent by the Museum of Mankind

Two are with stone tips and flights (6973), about 60 cm long. One is unflighted with a bone tip (NN Holmested). Fletcher draws 'one of their Arrows'.

j Scraping tool made by binding a mussel shell to a stone haft with a seal-hide lashing.
Tierra del Fuego. Probably *Yahgan*.

Length 20 cm
Lent by the Museum of Mankind, + 3556
(Presented by Francis Brent, Esq. FSA 1887)

This type of scraper was still in use among the *Yahgan* in the early part of the twentieth century, although the giant mussel shell was replaced whenever possible by a steel blade. Although principally a scraping tool, this type of artefact is also said to have been used as a hand-axe. A similar tool was also used by the *Ona*.

Fletcher's sketch has the caption 'The mussel shell whereof they make their knives & hatchetts.'

k Model canoe made of bark with two wooden paddles.
From Sandy Point, Straits of Magellan, Tierra del Fuego (Challenger Expedition). Probably *Yahgan*.
Length approx. 86 cm
Lent by the Museum of Mankind, + 756
(Presented by Sir Wyville Thomson.)

The *Chono, Alacaluf* and *Yahgan* all used bark canoes, and possibly also the *Ona*. These survived into the early part of the twentieth century but were gradually replaced by wooden boats. The *Yahgan* used the bark of the evergreen beech (*Nathofagus betuloides*) in the manufacture of their canoes. This was stripped from the trees in spring. The bark strips were sewn together with whalebone or split sapling wood and the seams wadded with stems of wild celery grass or moss mixed with mud. Although such canoes shipped water easily they were used for transport, including whaling expeditions.

Fletcher illustrates an Indian boat, captioned 'the manner of the Boates in all the Ilands to the Southward of America in the South Sea'. He describes them as made of 'large barke instead of other timber', and comments 'In all our travells in anny nation, we found not the like boates at anny tyme for forme and fine proportion'. Narborough illustrates Indian canoes, describing them as carrying ten or twelve people (**51**).

l Tightly coiled basket in grass.
Alacaluf, Tierra del Fuego.
Height 14 cm; diam. 10 cm
Lent by the Museum of Mankind, NN Holmested

m Coiled basket from Tierra del Fuego.
Suspended 25 cm; diam. 20 cm
Lent by the Museum of Mankind 55. 12–20. 187

Two of Narborough's Indian women hold baskets (**51**).

VII

The west coast of America

DRAKE'S course after his excursion south to Tierra del Fuego followed the instructions set out in the secret memorandum, that he was to sail north to 30°S, 'seeking along the said coast aforenamed . . . to find out places meet to have traffic for the venting of commodities of these her Majesty's realms. Whereas at present they are not under the obedience of any christian prince, so there is great hope of gold, silver, spices . . .'. That the 'aforenamed' coast was the coast of Chile is confirmed by the fact that Drake appointed latitude 30°S on the coast of Chile as the rendezvous with his consorts. A suggestion that the instructions referred to the coast of the southern continent can be ruled out. Neither Drake nor his promoters were interested in speculative exploring ventures on hypothetical coasts. The idea that Drake actually discovered the continent south-west of the Strait (a supposed discovery recorded on maps as late as the 1760s) can be traced to the displacement of the Tierra del Fuegan landfall westward on the maps of Levinus Hulsius (1602) and of Sir Robert Dudley in his *Dell' Arcano del Mare* Florence 1646–7, second edition, 1661. This mistake arose from the observation of the eclipse of the moon on 15 September 1578, from which the *Golden Hind*'s position was calculated to have been 90°W of London, as Cliffe recorded; whereas her true position must have been between 75° and 80°W.

Drake's immediate and ostensible objective, to establish trade relations with the Indians in an area believed to be outside the sphere of Spanish settlement, may be seen as a forerunner of Sir John Narborough's aims on his voyage of 1669–70. In fact the Spaniards had extended their activities further south than the English realized. The island of Mocha in 38°S where Drake made his first landfall (25 November 1578) was in the 'Tierra de Guerra', where the Spaniards were fighting the Indians for control. Sailing north from Mocha, Drake then sought a harbour suitable for the rendezvous, capturing *en route* a ship in the harbour of Valparaiso, and sacking the town. At Salado Bay in 27°55′S he spent a month overhauling the ship and waited in vain for the *Elizabeth* and *Marigold*. The next stage of the voyage comprised a campaign of piracy and plunder against the undefended Spanish ships and settlements on the coasts of Chile, Peru and Mexico. At Arica on 5 February 1578 he captured one ship and burnt another. At Chule he carried off an empty treasure ship. Arriving on 13 February at Callao, the port for Lima, capital of Peru and finding in the harbour thirty ships whose silver had been taken ashore, he cut their cables, chasing and capturing a ship which put in from Panama. His greatest prize was the treasure ship '*Nuestra Señora de la Concepción*', nicknamed the 'Cacafuego', captured off Cabo de San Francisco on 1 March as she sailed from Callao to Panama. In need of fresh supplies of water and of facilities to caulk and clean the *Golden Hind*, Drake sailed for the Nicaraguan coast, capturing on the way a bark with two pilots who had experience of the navigation to the Philippine Islands. After some days caulking the ship in a harbour opposite the island of Caño, Drake proceeded northward to the port of Guatulco in Mexico, plundered the town and robbed the church. Before he left on 16 April 1578, he released his prisoners.

The most circumstantial accounts of events on this extended plunder raid are provided by the testimonies of Drake's prisoners such as Nuño da Silva and San Juan de Anton, master of the 'Cacafuego'. To Gaspar de Vargas, Chief Alcade of Guatulco, Drake boasted that he had captured forty ships, large and small, and that only four of those he met escaped him. The Spanish pilot Pedro Sarmiento de Gamboa assessed the total of Drake's booty in silver and gold 'from the port of Valparaiso where he robbed the Capitana, called the *Los Reyes*, to Cabo de San Francisco, where he robbed San Juan de Anton', at 447,000 pesos *ensayados*, 'without counting the great quantity of plate, jewels of gold and silver, stones and some pearls . . . All these taken together, are estimated at more than one hundred thousand pesos . . .'. The full value of the booty will never be known; English officials were as amazed as the Spaniards were outraged, when Drake's takings were assessed in London and Seville (see **100, 104**). Drake gave his own version of his motives and objectives, one which tallied with the story he told his men in the harangue at Port St Julian (**48**): 'You will be saying now This man is a devil, who robs by day and prays at night in public. This is what I do, but it is just as when King Philip gives a very large written paper to your Viceroy . . . so the Queen, my Sovereign Lady, has ordered me to come to these parts . . . I am not going to stop until I have collected the two millions that my cousin John Hawkins lost, for certain, at San Juan de Ulua,' Drake asserted to Francisco Gomez Rengifo, factor of the port of Guatulco. The occasion of these remarks, the service which Gomez Rengifo was forced to attend as a prisoner on board, was itself an anti-Catholic demonstration with Foxe's *Book of Martyrs* (**32**) in central place. Nuño da Silva was to testify that after the capture of the 'Não Rica' (the *Nuestra Señora*) Drake told all his prisoners that he came in the service of the Queen, whose orders he carried and obeyed. Don Francisco de Zarate stated that Drake actually showed him the commissions from the Queen. There is, however, no evidence that Drake carried any sort of royal commission. The plunder-raid itself went beyond the instructions in the secret memorandum, which could not be expected to specify an objective with such serious political implications. The instructions clearly left scope for Drake to convert the voyage into a privateering raid, his main objective. His confidence that in the eyes of the promoters handsome profits would 'make' the voyage and outweigh any diplomatic scruples, proved well founded.

With the voyage 'made', and the *Golden Hind* heavy with treasure, Drake's aim was to find the safest and shortest way home. His various statements to the prisoners about his intended route, made in the knowledge that such reports would be relayed to the Viceroy, must be interpreted with caution. Despite the belief of certain Spanish officials that Drake would return by the Strait, and their hasty counter-measures (**53**), Drake would not risk the danger of capture off the South American coast, as Sarmiento surmised. 'They said that they were going to return straight to their country by the Molucca route', the captured pilot Alonso Sanchez Colchero reported, alleging that Drake had ordered him to pilot the ship on the 'China' route. Nuño da Silva asserted, on the contrary, that Drake had told him and other prisoners that he was bound to return by the Strait 'de Bacallaos' which he had come to discover and that, failing to find an exit through the said Strait, he was bound to return by China.

Drake's course northward to California leaves the matter an open question. He needed to find a harbour to repair and refit before making the return voyage, whether westward bound for the Moluccas or northward by way of the north-west passage. In the event he sailed as far north as 42°N (the Anonymous Account gives 48°N), in which latitude Ortelius's world map of 1564 and Gilbert's derived map of 1576 showed the Strait of Anian opening out eastward into the north-west passage round North America. Finding the coast to continue northwards, and 'being afraid to spend long time in seeking for the straite' (as the author of the 'Anonymous Narrative' records (**68**), Drake turned south, now determined on the route to the Moluccas. In 38°N he found a suitable harbour where he stayed for six weeks, from 17 June to 23 July 1579. After a ceremony in which the Indians of the region crowned him and apparently handed over sovereignty of their country, he took formal possession of the territory on behalf of Queen Elizabeth, naming it Nova Albion. At the end of July 1579 the *Golden Hind* set sail south-westward for the Moluccas. She was now westward bound on the completion of the second circumnavigation of the world, although the voyage originally had not been planned as such.

Despite the secrecy which surrounded the voyage on Drake's return, Richard Hakluyt was quick to add Drake's discoveries on the 'backside' of America to the record of English activities in North America (see **11, 73**). The various maps celebrating the circumnavigation, based on the large map which Drake gave to the Queen (the Whitehall map, **99**), gave a general impression of Drake's course and discoveries in Nova Albion, although only that by Hondius, *ca* 1595 (in its inset 'Portus Novæ Albionis') provided topographical detail (see **74, 75, 76, 78, 79, 88**). The act of possession likewise was seized upon by the colonial entrepreneurs. Stephen Parmenius, the Hungarian friend of Hakluyt's, and companion of Gilbert on his fateful colonizing voyage of 1582, made allusion to it in his Latin poem, printed by Hakluyt in 1600 (III.142) with the marginal note 'Nova Albion'. In free translation, America was stretching out her right hand and offering her power and faith to the indomitable Britons. When Sir Walter Raleigh planted in 1585 on the coast of Virginia (now North Carolina) the first English colony on American soil, Drake's act of possession took on a further significance. England's claim by title of priority of discovery to northern North America was reinforced. The colonists of the later Virginia colony, whose bounds by charter reached from sea to sea, were encouraged in their explorations westward in the 1650s by their belief in the right to possession of the Pacific coast of North America (**81**).

61 Ortelius's world map of 1564

Nova totius terrarum orbis iuxta neotericorum traditiones descriptio. Abrah. Ortelio Anverpiano auct. Anno Domini M.CCCCC.LXIIII.
Antwerp, 1564.
8 sh. 44 × 37 cm   *Maps C.2.a.6*

Ortelius's large world map of 1564 appears to have been known in London in the 1560s, as Humphrey Gilbert copied it in a much reduced form to illustrate his *Discourse of a Discouerie for a new Passage to Cataia*, (1576). The fact that the 1564 map depicts the north-west passage as an easy and open route, in contrast to the much less encouraging indications on Ortelius's world map of 1570, explains why Drake is conjectured to have had a copy with him, although the generally northern trend of the coast of Chile seems contrary evidence (see **44, 62**). Insets display views of Cuzco and Tenochtitlán, the capital cities of the Inca empire in Peru and the Aztec empire in Mexico, the Kingdoms of the Sun.

62 Ortelius's World Map of 1570

Abraham Ortelius 'Typus Orbis Terrarum'.
Franciscus Hogenbergus sculpsit.
From *Theatrum Orbis Terrarum*, 1579.
MS additions. 34 × 49 cm   *920.(327)*

Abraham Ortelius's world map published in his *Theatrum Orbis Terrarum* (1570) and its many later editions can be regarded as the best known world map of the sixteenth century. This issue of 1579 has been annotated in MS with Drake's track. A note in French on Tierra del Fuego records Drake's discovery of the 'Elizabethides'. The north-west trend of the coast of Chile from the Strait of Magellan explains why Drake twice set a course north-west for Peru. Although Fletcher, in pointing to this error of the 'generall mappes', referred to 'false and fraudulent coniectures', the distortion can be attributed to the map-makers' difficulty in compiling maps from charts showing the same coasts in different longitudes. Thus Sancho Gutiérrez's manuscript chart of the Pacific, 1551, shows Chile with two coastlines, one many degrees to the west of the other.

It is probable that Drake had a copy of Ortelius's map with him.

63 Drake in the South Sea

'William Hack: To the Right: Honourable John Lord Sommers ... This following Description of the Coast & Islands &c in the South Sea of America is most humbly dedicated ... 1698.'
MS coloured on paper. 44 cm
K.Mar.VIII.16.(7 tab. 122)

The Spaniards recorded their surveys of the Pacific coast of the Americas and their sailing directions in manuscript volumes known as *derroteros*, which they treated as highly secret documents. It was not until the late seventeenth century that one of these, captured by Bartholomew Sharp in 1680, became available for use in England. Copied out in English translation by William Hack into fine bound volumes, these were then presented to royal personages and high officials of the day. Charts from Hack's Atlas of 1698 illustrate better than the smaller scale maps of his own time Drake's activities on the west coast of America. The main change lay in the forts built in reaction to Drake's raids, to protect the ports from further foreign interlopers.

a   'Valparayso' (map 134)

At the Bay of Quintero Drake obtained intelligence from a Spanish-speaking Indian named Felipe that a ship lay in the harbour at Valparaiso, fifteen miles south. Turning back southward with the Indian as guide, he reached Valparaiso on 5 December 1578, and here made his first raid on a Spanish American port. He captured the *Los Reyes*, called by the English the *Capitana*, which had been Sarmiento de Gamboa's ship on his voyage of discovery to the Solomon Islands in 1568. Drake then went on shore and sacked the town, comprising some eight or nine houses, and the church. The booty from the ship amounted to 25,000 *pesos* of fine Valdivia gold to the value of 37,000 ducats (Anonymous Narrative), and 'a great crosse of gold beset with Emeraulds on which was nailed a God of the same metall' (*World Encompassed*, p. 41). The Spaniards later claimed the gold to value 100m pesos. Drake carried the prize with him using the ship's master, a Greek named Juan, as pilot to guide him. He also had the benefit of the sea chart of the pilot of the *Capitana*, as Sarmiento reports.

b   41'Callao' (map 97).

On his arrival (13 February) at Callao, the port for Lima, capital of Peru, Drake found about thirty ships in the harbour, but was told that the silver had been taken ashore. A ship which put in from Panama was chased and captured, and at the same time Drake's men cut the cables of all the ships in the harbour. When the Viceroy sent two ships in pursuit, Drake used the prize as a decoy and made good his escape.

c   'Panama Bay' (map 51).

At Callao Drake had heard that the ship *Nuestra Señora de la Concepción* had left Callao for Panama fourteen days ahead of him. 'That gallant shippe the *Cacafuego*, the great glory of the South Sea' now became Drake's quarry, and a chain of gold was promised to the first man who sighted her. On 28 February near Cape San Francisco at the entrance to Panama Bay Drake captured the ship of Benito Diaz Bravo, transferred her treasure of gold, silver, and emeralds, and set her adrift. Off Punta de la Galera the *Cacafuego* was sighted by

became confused in the telling, for it would have been more logical for the *Golden Hind* to have been called the *Cacafuego*, and for an Englishman to make the parting riposte, that the *Golden Hind* was now the *Caca Plata*.

65 Deposition of San Juan de Anton

San Juan de Anton m[r] and owner of a shippe called Nra Señora de la Concecion being comannded by D. Alonso Criado, cheefe Judge of the Royal Court of Panama, the sixt[h] of the month of March 1579, to depose uppon his othe what he knoweth touching his being spoyled by certen Englishmen in this Sea of Sur of such treasure as he was laden wth all for his M[trs] and for certen other pryvat persons The said Juan de Anton sayeth as followeth.

MS 32 cm   *Lent by the P.R.O. SP 94/1. no. 23A.*

San Juan de Anton's deposition made before the Judge at Panama on 16 March 1579 records the capture of the *Nuestra Señora de la Concepción* on 22 January 1578, and the seizure of her cargo of silver valued at '360,000 pesos more or lesse'. From conversations with Drake himself and with the other prisoners (notably Nuño de Silva) San Juan, during his six days on board the *Golden Hind*, was able to obtain a general account of the voyage and details of Drake's attacks on Spanish ports and shipping along the coasts of Chile and Peru. The report that Drake was greatly feared by his men and that he had a guard about his person (f. 76[r]) is also noted. To Anton's questions on his intended course homeward, Drake answered that there were three ways, 'by Cabo de buena esperanza (the Cape of Good Hope) towards China', by Chile the way he had come, and he would not reveal the third way.

San Juan's testimony with other depositions and a derived document dated 15 April 1578 were the first official reports of Drake's activities to reach Spain. From these papers statements were prepared and sent to England as a basis for the claim against Drake. This document is a contemporary English translation of San Juan's deposition.

Caca Fogo. *Caca Plata.*

John Drake, who received the reward of the gold chain. The *Golden Hind* sailed in pursuit, overhauled and captured the *Cacafuego* on 1 March 1579.

64 The capture of the 'Cacafuego'

Levinus Hulsius: *Sechster Theil, Kurze Warhafftige Relation unnd Beschreibung der Wunderbarsten Vier Schiffahrten so jemals verricht worden.* Franckfurt, 1602.

19 cm   *C.114.c.21*

Hulsius's engraving (pl. xv) shows the *Golden Hind* on 1 March coming alongside to starboard of the *Nuestra Señora de la Concepción*, nicknamed the 'Cacafuego' (which may be euphemistically translated 'Spit'fire). Ordered to surrender, the Master San Juan de Anton answered 'What old tub is that which orders me to strike sail? Come on board and strike sail yourselves!' In reply, Drake fired a volley into the Cacafuego, and the pinnace landed men on the port side. Unarmed, Anton surrendered his ship. The whole cargo transferred to the *Golden Hind* comprised gold, silver bars and silver coin to the value of 362,000 pesos, of which 106,000 belonged to the King. Drake then released the ship and her men. 'Our ship shall no more be called the Cacafuego, but the Cacaplata. Your ship shall be called the Cacafuego', someone shouted from the Spanish ship as they parted. (Hulsius, p. 15.) The names Caca Fogo and Caca Plata ('Spit'silver) appear in the engraving. The story perhaps

66 Losses of an English merchant in Mexico

Travels of John Chilton.

30 cm   *Additional MS 22904, f. 8*

Among those who suffered losses at Drake's hand through his robberies at Guatulco was one of his own countrymen, John Chilton. An English merchant who for seventeen or eighteen years (1568–86) lived and travelled in the West Indies and Central America, Chilton records thus the incident at Guatulco: 'Here S[r] Frauncis Drake arrived in the yere 79 in the month of Aprill, by whose comyng thither I loste above 1000 ducketts wch he tooke (wth much other goodes of divers other marchauntes of Mexico) from one Francisco Gomis Rangifa, factor at that time for all Spanish marchauntes that then traded in ye South Sea, for in this porte, they use to shipp all the goodes wch they transport to the Peru, and the Kingdome of Hunduras.' The factor Francisco Gomez Rengifo, who had goods at his house awaiting trans-shipment, was captured by the boatswain and taken to the ship. From his home they stole everything that it contained belonging to him and to others (including Chilton), which amounted to about 7,000 pesos in reals, silver and gold and in clothing.

The manuscript is in the hand of a copyist, but with a few corrections (including 'S^r Fr. Drak' in the margin of this page) which may be *autograph*. It was printed by Hakluyt in the *Principal Navigations* (1598–1600), III, 457.

67 Charting new worlds

[A chart of the north-west coast of Mexico and the Californian peninsula.]
In an atlas of eighteen charts drawn by Joan Martines of Messina in 1578.
MS coloured. 24 × 36 cm
Harley MS 3450, map 10

Joan Martines, a map-maker of Spanish descent who worked at Messina, is famous for the series of fine and beautifully decorated atlases dated between 1556 and 1591, with maps drawn in the ornate style of the Majorcan school. The atlases were intended not for use in navigation, but for presentation to notable and wealthy personages of the day. In this map of the north-west coast of America, Martines evidently used among his sources the maps of Baptista Agnese and the world map of Ortelius, 1564 (see **49, 61**). A northern strait separates North America from Asia, with Japan straddling the narrow North Pacific ocean as on Ortelius's map. The legendary Seven Cities of Civola are shown in resplendent detail.

68 Exploits in California

A discourse of Sir Francis Drakes iorney and exploytes after hee had past ye Straytes of Magellan into Mare de Sur, and through the rest of his voyadge afterward till hee arived in England. 1580 anno.
20 cm
Harley MS 280. f. 87^r-v

Known as the 'Anonymous Narrative', the text begins with the landfall at the Island of Mocha. For the course after Guatulco, this is the leading authority for the assumption that Drake was seeking the north-west passage for his return route. Drake is reported to have

sailed north to 48°N, where 'still finding a very lardge sea trending toward the north, but being afraid to spend long time in seeking for the straite, hee turned back againe, still keping along the cost, as nere land as hee might, untill hee came to 44.gt, and the hee found a harborow for his ship.' There Drake set up a 'greate post', on which he nailed 'a plate of lead, and scratched therein the Queenes name'.

The author of 'The Famous Voyage' used this manuscript as his source for events as far as Guatulco. References to a quarrel with William Legge at Ternate and critical details of other dealings between them explain Corbett's attribution of authorship to Legge.

69 Drake's crowning by the Californian Indians

Arnoldus Montanus: *De Nieuwe en Onbekende Weereld: of Beschryving van America en t'Zuid-Land*. Amsterdam, 1671.
32 cm   *984.h.13*

Arnoldus Montanus (Tweede Boek, p. 213) here depicts the ceremony of 26 June 1579 in 'Portus Novæ Albionis'; Drake is being 'crowned' with an Indian headdress by the chief of the Indians who had arrived from further afield with a guard of about 100 men. 'The King himselfe . . . joyfully singing a Song, set the Crowne upon his head; enriched his necke with all their Chaines; and offering unto him many other things, honoured him by the name of Hyóh.' (*The World Encompassed*, p. 61.) The Englishmen naively assumed that the Indians in so doing were surrendering 'their right and Title in the whole Land', becoming Drake's vassals 'in themselves and their posterities'. In this spirit Drake graciously 'tooke the Scepter, Crowne, and Dignity, of the said Country into his hand'.

Arnoldus Montanus was the grandson of Petrus Montanus and of Jacomina, Jodocus Hondius's sister. This family connection (Petrus Montanus was a partner in the firm of Hondius) has led one authority to assume that this view was based on documentary sources, and to describe it as the first landscape to show identifiable shoreline features of San Francisco Bay (see **78**).

70 Drake's Act of Possession in Nova Albion

The World Encompassed By Sir Francis Drake . . . Carefully collected out of the notes of Master Francis Fletcher Preacher in this imployment, and divers others his followers in the same.
21 cm   *G.6519*

'This country our generall named Albion . . . Before we went from thence, our generall caused to be set up, a Monument of our being there, as also of her Majesties, and successors right and title to that kingdome, namely, a Plate of Brasse, fast nailed to a great and firme post . . .' (p. 80). Granted the title to Nova Albion (as he supposed) in the ceremony of crowning by the Indians (**69**), Drake in this act took formal possession of Nova Albion, named from the white banks and cliffs along the shore and from the Greek name for England, Albion (which John Dee still used). The white cliffs are identified as the fine line of chalk cliffs of Point Reyes and Drakes Bay – a striking landmark for ships.

This was Drake's second recorded act of possession, and the first on the mainland of North America. It is significant that he made these claims of possession on behalf of the English Crown at his most southerly and most northerly landing places, Elizabeth Island in 56°S (see **57**), and 'Portus Novæ Albionis' in 38°N. In Nova Albion, 'the Spaniards never had any dealing, or so much as set a foote in this country; the utmost of their discoveries, reaching onely to many degrees Southward of this place'.

Although *The World Encompassed* carries a letter of dedication to the Earl of Warwick written by Drake's nephew, Sir Francis Drake (Bart.), the identity of the author remains unknown.

71 Portus Novæ Albionis and the plate of brass

Sir Francis Drake's Plate of Brass.
Navigators Guild, Point Reyes, California.
13.5 × 20 cm   *Map Library*

For the identification of the 'convenient and fit harbrough' in about 38°N where the *Golden Hind* came to anchor and remained from 17 June until 23 July 1579, the major piece of evidence is the inset plan entitled 'Portus Novæ Albionis' in Jodocus Hondius's 'Broadside' Map *ca* 1596 (**78**). This shows the *Golden Hind* anchored at the head of a small bay with an Indian settlement on shore. On the assumption that the latitude was about 38°N, three possible sites have been considered, Bodega Bay in 38°20′N, Drakes Bay in 38°N, and a bay within San Francisco Bay, entered through the Golden Gate in 37°49′N. Sailing south from 43°N Drake would first discover Bodega Bay, but the absence of white cliffs (see **70**) has been suggested as evidence against this identification. If the cliffs were in the immediate vicinity of 'Portus Novæ Albionis', then Drake's anchorage was presumably within Drakes Bay (as it is now called), and would be identified with Drake's Estero, although the entrance to this is now closed by a bar and silt. This identification was favoured by the late Admiral S. E. Morison on his reconnaissance voyage of 1973, and is promoted by the Drake Navigators Guild. For the third site, San Francisco Bay, the problem is to explain the lack of any report in the narratives of the discovery of a great bay or gulf (one which presumably would have seemed like the entrance to the north-west passage). A new piece of evidence apparently in favour of San Francisco Bay came to light when a plate of brass inscribed with the facts of Drake's act of possession was found in 1936 in Marin County on a hill overlooking the south face of Point San Quentin, San Francisco Bay. The hole (to the right) presumably contained the silver sixpence bearing the Queen's head and arms. Now preserved in the Bancroft Library, Berkeley, the plate of brass aroused great publicity at the time of its discovery, and in the course of the proceedings a chauffeur claimed to have found the plate on a roadside near Drakes Bay. Against the authenticity of the plate of brass is the form of the lettering, spelling and language, none of which is typical of the sixteenth century. This fact suggests that the plate may be a forgery made to fit the information given in *The World Encompassed*. It should also be noted that the 'Anonymous Narrative' (**68**) refers to 'a plate of lead', on which the Queen's name was scratched.

72 North-west coast Indian artefacts

a Grass basket-work bowl: from Santa Barbara, California. Probably from a Hokan Indian group.
Diam. 23 cm   *Van. 181*

b Bow: composite recurved bow from Trinidada, Monterey, California. Probably from a Penutian Indian group.
Length 86.5 cm   *Van. 4*

c Arrow with a flint point: from Monterey, California(?). Probably from a Penutian Indian group.
Length 84.5 cm   *Van. 18*
Lent by the B.M. Museum of Mankind from the Hewett-Vancouver collection presented by A. W. Franks in 1891.

The Indians Drake met in Nova Albion were probably members of the Coast Miwok tribe who lived in an area roughly bounded by Cape Mendocino to the north and San Francisco Bay to the south. No artefacts from these people survive in British collections. The present items dating from the eighteenth century are among the earliest surviving aboriginal material from California and illustrate types of weapons and containers which would have been in use there at a much earlier date. These three pieces were collected on the voyage of Captain George Vancouver 1790–5.

73 Hakluyt records Drake's American Discoveries

Novus Orbis. [Engraved by] 'P.G.'
In: Richard Hakluyt *De Orbe Novo*, Paris, 1587.
17 × 20 cm   *C.45.b.10*

Richard Hakluyt illustrated his edition (1587) of Peter Martyr's *Decades of the New World*, the celebrated history of Spain's American empire, with a map of America which the engraver dedicated to Hakluyt and in the decorative border signed 'P.G.' (probably Philipp Galle). Evidently based on a Spanish source, as the prime meridian is through Toledo, the map displays details of Drake's discoveries, for which record Hakluyt was no doubt responsible. Off South America an archipelago is depicted with the legend 'Ins. Reginae Elisabethæ 1579 ab Anglis', and open sea beyond. In the north-west of the continent appears 'Nova Albion inventa an. 1580. ab Anglis'. It is significant that as on the map in Hakluyt's '*Divers Voyages*' (1582; see **11**) Drake himself is not named.

74 The Drake silver medal, 1589

Micha: Merca: fecit extat Londi: prope templum Gallo: An° 1589.
Diam. 6.8 cm   *Lent by Hans P. Kraus*

The Drake silver medal or map became known in the later years of the nineteenth century as an anonymous and undated record of Drake's voyage, surviving in three or perhaps four examples. A possible clue to its authorship was provided by Samuel Purchas in *Purchas his Pilgrimes* (1625): 'my learned friend Master Brigges told me, that he hath seene this plot of Drakes Voyage cut in Silver by a Dutchman (Michael Mercator, Nephew to Gerardus) many years before Scouten or Maire intended that voyage' (*i.e.* many years before 1615). This unique and hitherto unknown example of the medal bearing Michael Mercator's inscription appeared in Christie's London salerooms in April, 1967, as the property of the Earl of Caledon. The legend reads: 'Michael Mercator made [this.] It is available in London near the French Church, 1589'.

Michael Mercator (*ca* 1567–1614) was the son of Arnold Mercator (1537–1587), the grandson (not nephew) of Gerard Mercator the elder, and first cousin to the younger Gerard Mercator. Poll tax returns show that Michael Mercator was in London in 1590, being assessed in June of that year as 'servaunte to Baptista...' of 'St. Bennet Finckes Paroche'. The French Huguenot Church (*templum*) was St Bernard's Church on the corner of Threadneedle Street.

This example of the silver medal therefore ranks as the earliest extant dated map of Drake's voyage. For the configuration and placenames of America and the Pacific coast Mercator copied the map engraved by 'P.G.' in

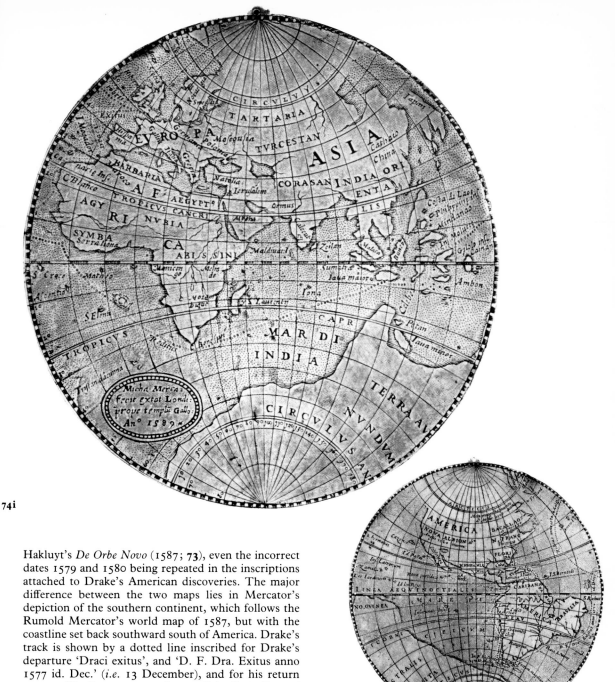

74i

74ii

Hakluyt's *De Orbe Novo* (1587; **73**), even the incorrect dates 1579 and 1580 being repeated in the inscriptions attached to Drake's American discoveries. The major difference between the two maps lies in Mercator's depiction of the southern continent, which follows the Rumold Mercator's world map of 1587, but with the coastline set back southward south of America. Drake's track is shown by a dotted line inscribed for Drake's departure 'Draci exitus', and 'D. F. Dra. Exitus anno 1577 id. Dec.' (*i.e.* 13 December), and for his return voyage 'Reditus anno 1580, 4 Cal. Oc.' (*i.e.* 26 September).

Of the nine Drake medals now known to survive, this one was presumably the prototype. The author's inscription was probably omitted on the later medals for patriotic reasons as the medal thus inscribed gave prominence to Mercator and gave Drake only passing reference in the legends recording his departure. An eastern hemisphere (lacking the inscription) is preserved in the Bagford Collection and has been recently identified as the only known example on paper (*i.e.* a counter-impression) (**96**).

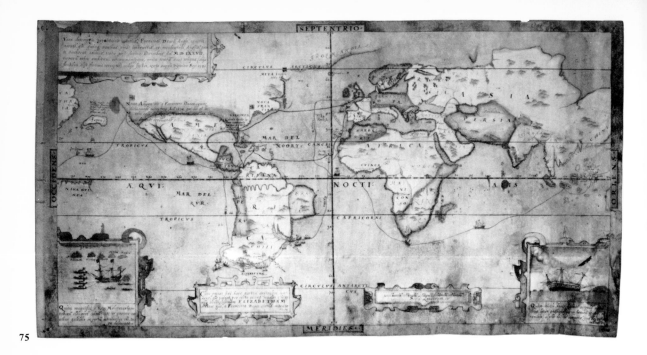

75 The Drake–Mellon Map

Vera descriptio expeditionis nauticæ, Francisci
Draci Angli, cognitis aurati, qui quinque navibus
probe instructis, ex occidentali Anglia parte
anchoras soluens, tertio post decimo Decembris
Anᵒ M.D.LXXVII, terraru[m] orbis ambitum
circumnavigans, unica tentu navi reliqua (alijs
fluctibus, alijs flamina correptis) redux factus,
sexto supra Vigesimo Sep: 1580.
MS; drawn after 1586.
> *Photograph of the original (24 × 45 cm) in the
> collection of Mr Paul Mellon.*

The manuscript map known after its present owner as
the Drake–Mellon map is notable as one of the closest
extant copies of the map which Drake presented to
Queen Elizabeth, and which Purchas recorded as 'still
hanging in His Maiesties Gallerie at Whitehall, neere
the Privie Chamber' (*Purchas his Pilgrimes* (1625), Part
III, lib iii, pp. 461–2). The legend about the discovery of
Elizabeth Island below South America on the Mellon
map follows almost word for word the text quoted by
Purchas. Insets illustrate two incidents of the voyage,
the reception at the Moluccas and the *Golden Hind* stuck
on the reef at Celebes.

The map must have been drawn *ca* 1587 or later, as it
displays the track of Drake's West Indian voyage
(1585–6) as well as that of the circumnavigation. Flags of
St George at Elizabeth Island and Nova Albion assert
England's claims through Drake's two acts of
possession, and the legend proclaiming the discovery of
Nova Albion and its cession to the Queen is correctly

dated 1579 (*cf.* **78, 97**). On the eastern shore of the North
American continent a third flag flies over the Virginia
colony of Sir Walter Raleigh (founded 1585), and a
fourth represents Frobisher's act of possession (1576) in
Meta Incognita (Baffin Island). The indication of the
north boundary of New Spain gives the impression
(intentional or otherwise) that the north parts of North
America now lie open to England's imperial designs.

76 The Molyneux globes, 1592

[Terrestrial globe:] Anno Domini 1603 Emerius
⁣   Mulleneux Angl' sumptibus
⁣   Gulielmi Sandersoni
⁣   Londinensis descripsit.
[Celestial:] Iodocus Hondius Flan. sc. 1592.
London, 1592. Second edition issued in
Amsterdam, 1603.
Diam. 62 cm
Lent by the Honourable Society of the Middle Temple

The pair of globes by Emery Molyneux published in
London in 1592 were the first globes printed in England
and the first to be made by an Englishman. The
terrestrial provides a detailed record of England's
achievements in exploration, navigation and discovery.
Foremost and most spectacular among these were the
recent circumnavigations of Drake and Cavendish, and
Drake's West Indian voyage. The globe is the earliest
surviving work to show the tracks of both circumnavigations, and records the events of the voyages in detail,
with suitable comments. The celestial globe is a copy of
Mercator's of 1551, with the addition of the new constel-

76

lations, the Southern Cross and the Southern Triangle, for which Molyneux followed the Dutch globe of Jacob van Langeren, 1589, designed by Peter Plancius.

In his *Principall Navigations* (1589), Hakluyt heralded the publication of the terrestrial globe, to which Shakespeare also referred in *The Comedy of Errors* (III.ii). The globes were financed by the merchant adventurer, William Sanderson, who spent more than £1000 on them. At his house in Newington-Butts, two special entertainments were held, at which first the terrestrial, and then the celestial were presented to the Queen. Molyneux, a mathematician of Lambeth, was assisted in the construction of the globes by the mathematician Edward Wright and by Jodocus Hondius as engraver. An emigré from the Netherlands resident in London from 1583–4, Hondius returned to the Netherlands in 1593, and was followed there by Molyneux in 1596 or 1597, one or other taking with him the copper-plates of the globes. The terrestrial of the Middle Temple pair was revised by Hondius, with the original date 1592 altered to 1603, and the addition of recent discoveries. Only one example of the terrestrial globe in its original state survives (at Petworth House). The globes at the Middle Temple were first acquired by William Crashaw, who was preacher there from 1605 to 1613, and had in his private library 'one of the fairest paire of globes in Englande'. He probably presented the globes to the Middle Temple in 1613 among his other donations.

77 A Treatise on the Molyneux globes and Drake's voyage

M. Blundevile His Exercises, London, 1594.
19 cm   *C.145.c.16*

The second part of Thomas Blundeville's Exercises comprised *A plaine description of Mercator his two Globes . . . Whereunto is added a briefe description of the two great Globes lately set foorth by M. Molinaxe: and of Sir Frances Drake his first voyage into the Indies*. Blundeville (ff. 242ᵛ–244ʳ) describes Drake's voyage as depicted by the track (a red line) on the terrestrial globe. He gives Drake's most northerly point in Nova Albion as 46°N, and suggests that Drake would have liked to have sailed home by the north-west passage (so Blundeville has heard), 'but his Mariners finding the coast of Nova Albion to be very cold, had no good will to sayle any further Northward.' Finally, it would greatly profit Drake's countrymen, Blundeville concludes, 'if it might please Sir Frances to write a perfect Diarie of his whole voyage . . . and thereby deserue immortall fame . . . of all which things, I doubt not but that he hath alreadie written, and will publish the same when he shall thinke most meete'.

A friend of John Dee and Edward Wright, Blundeville was educated at Cambridge and wrote his *Exercises* and other works for the instruction of young gentlemen, especially those at the Inns of Court.

78 The Drake 'Broadside' Map by Jodocus Hondius, 1595

Vera totius expeditionis nauticæ descriptio D. Franc. Draci . . . Addita est etiam viva delineatio navigationes Thomæ Caundish . . . Iudocus Hondius. Amsterdam, *ca* 1595.
With accompanying text.
38 × 54 cm   *M.T.6.a.2*

Sometimes known as the 'Hondius Broadside' on account of the accompanying Dutch text, this map was engraved by Jodocus Hondius probably after his return to the Netherlands in 1593. The text comprises a version of the 'Famous Voyage' and of Cavendish's circumnavigation taken from Hakluyt's *Principall Navigations* (1589), and includes portraits of Drake and Cavendish, inset with hemispheric world maps. That of Drake, inscribed 'Aet. suæ 43', erroneously displays Cavendish's track. The publication of the Dutch text in 1596 as a separate pamphlet with similar accompanying portraits suggests that the Broadside Map was published in Amsterdam about 1595. As engraver of the Molyneux globes, Hondius had had access to sources for the routes of the circumnavigations (and may well have had the plates of the globes with him in Amsterdam; see 76). He presumably also knew the Whitehall map or a derivative, in view of the similarities between his map and the other maps believed to be based on the Whitehall map.

The Hondius Broadside map is of special interest for the four insets, two of which are similar to those in the Mellon and the Van Sype maps (75, 97). The other two show 'Portus Novæ Albionis' in Nova Albion and 'Portus Javæ Majoris' (illustrated). These are notable as the only details of local topography to survive in printed contemporary records.

Five other examples of the map are now known.

79 Edward Wright's world map, 1599

Thou hast here . . . a true hydrographical description of so much of the world as hath beene hetherto discouered, and is comme to our knowledge . . . .
In: Richard Hakluyt *Principal Navigations*, vol. I (1598–1600).
47 × 65 cm   *683.h.5*

Although the world chart included in Hakluyt's *Principal Navigations* was known for many years as the Molyneux, or Hakluyt-Molyneux map because of its similarity to Molyneux's terrestrial globe, 1592, it is now identified as the work of Edward Wright the mathematician. The map is drawn on Mercator's projection which Edward Wright adapted using a mathematical formula. Wright is also now known as the author of a similar map published in the second edition

of Wright's *Certaine errors in Navigation* (1610). As Molyneux's collaborator in the production of the globes (see 76), Wright was well placed to reduce the globe to map form, whereas Molyneux removed to the Netherlands in 1596 or 1597 and died between June 1598 and April 1599.

The map was famous in its day, for Shakespeare alludes to it in *Twelfth Night*, III.ii, where Maria says of Malvolio: 'He does smile his face into more lines than are in the new map, with the augmentation of the Indies' (references to the compass lines and (presumably) to the islands discovered by the Spaniards – the Solomon Islands – stretching eastwards from New Guinea).

The second state of the map (exhibited) includes an additional legend in the south-east Pacific, recording Drake's discovery that Tierra del Fuego was an archipelago and that the coast of Chile trended not north-westward but east of north.

80 A German version of Drake's map

Theodore de Bry: *Americæ Pars VIII. Continens primo, descriptionem trium itinerum Nobilissimi et fortissimi equitis Francisca Draken, qui peragrato primum universo terrarum orbe* . . . Frankfurt, 1599.
34 × 52 cm   *C.115.h.3.(3)*

In his celebrated collection of voyages Theodor de Bry includes, in the Latin and the German editions of *America Part VIII*, an account of Drake's circumnavigation abridged from Hakluyt (1589). The title page displays a map of the voyage in two hemispheres closely resembling that of Hondius, *ca* 1595 (78), and decorated with Drake's portrait as well as a picture of the *Golden Hind*.

81 Ten days march west of Virginia

A mapp of Virginia discouered to yᵉ Hills . . . Domina Virginia Farrer Collegit. John Goddard sculp. London, 1651.
In: Edward Bland *The Discovery of New Brittaine*, 1651.
30 × 38 cm   *278.a.3*

John Farrer, an agent of the Virginia Company, illustrates in this map the misconception that the Pacific Ocean lay not far beyond the hills of tide-water Virginia. In this issue the word 'hills' has been altered (on the plate) from 'falls', found in an earlier state of the map. Sir Francis Drake's discovery and act of possession in Nova Albion, complete with portrait, is represented as ten days' march from the head of the James River.

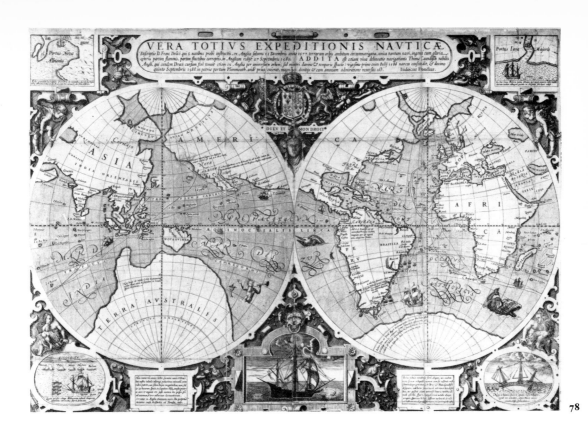

78

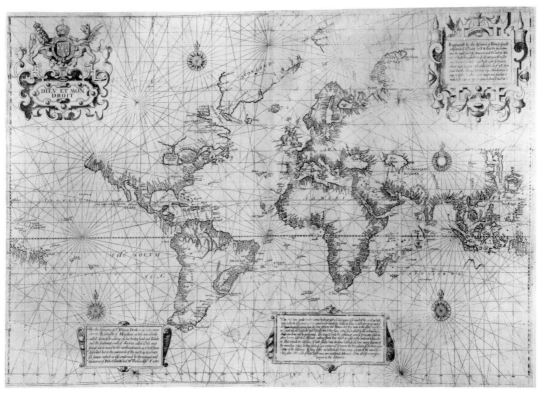

79

VIII

To the Spice Islands and home

DRAKE'S main concern on leaving the Californian coast was to return home as quickly and safely as possible. He did not however intend to miss the opportunity of trade with the Moluccan islands, and although apparently making for Tidore, he was soon persuaded by the Sultan of Ternate to anchor instead at his port. As the greater part of the clove trade was under the Sultan's control, and as he was continually at war with the Portuguese who then held Tidore, he and Drake soon came to a mutually beneficial arrangement. After some ceremonious haggling and despite bad feeling, at which a few of the chroniclers hint, it seems that an agreement was reached. In exchange presumably for English protection at sea (Drake boasted he would decorate the seas with English ships) the clove trade, subject to the Sultan's usual commission, would be given exclusively to the English. Although this was conveniently cited later as a formal agreement by the nascent East India Company, it seems unlikely that Drake was empowered to conclude any such treaty by the Queen. Indeed in the surviving plan for the voyage a visit to the Moluccas was not even envisaged and Drake was supposed to return home through the Strait of Magellan.

Drake left Ternate with a cargo of cloves, some of which he had to throw overboard when his ship struck a reef off the east coast of Celebes. As is evident from contemporary maps, both Portuguese and Spanish, the shape and position of Celebes (and most of the other islands in the East Indies) were not understood. Neither did Drake, as far as is known, have local pilots on board once past Ternate. The course he took was tortuous in the extreme. He was forced south by contrary winds and then east far into the Banda Sea. It is uncertain whether he had originally intended to sail south of Java and the adjacent islands to avoid the northern Portuguese routes from Malacca and Bantam to the Moluccan Islands. But by doing so he clearly demonstrated to his own satisfaction at least that Java was an island and was not joined to the continent of *Terra Australis*, still apparently a problem for the Dutch when Cornelis Houtman sailed round the island on his voyage of 1596.

On his return Drake was greeted with almost universal acclaim. As an anonymous commentator wryly remarked in 1582 Drake 'was so well welcome, and so liberall in the devision of shares to some Courtiers that notwithstanding the gallowes claimed his interest . . . he was at Deptford rewarded with the honor of Knight-hoode, and in the same ship, wherewith he had bene abrode a roving . . . Only the ones who stole too little suffer.'

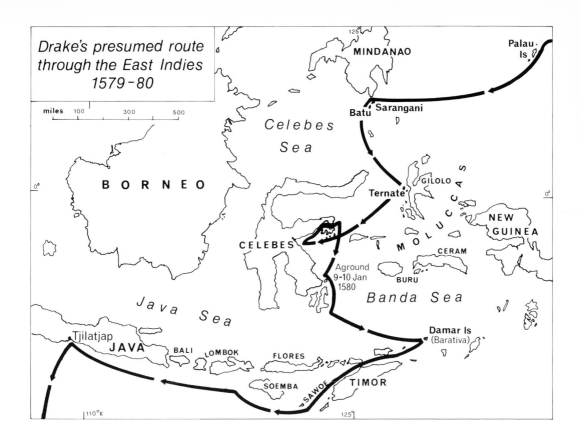

Drake's presumed route through the East Indies 1579–80

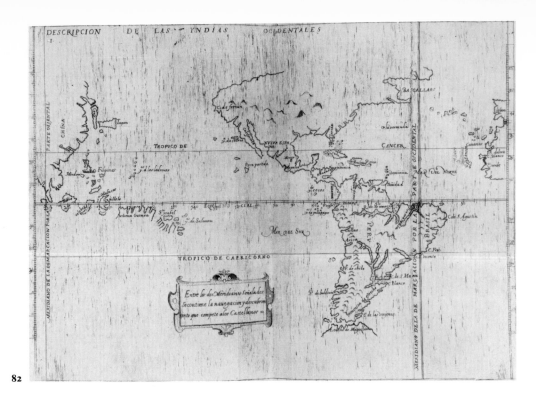

82

82   The Pacific Crossing

Descripcion de las Yndias Ocidentalis.
[Map of the Pacific Ocean showing the West Coast
of America and the coast of China and the East
Indies.]
In: Antonio de Herrera *Descripcion de las Indias
Occidentales*. Madrid, 1601–15.
21 × 30 cm   *K.Top. CXVIII.2–a*

On 25 July 1579 Drake set sail from the Farallones (St
James Islands) for the Moluccas. John Drake briefly
recorded the crossing in 1587 for the Inquisition in
Lima and made reference to the Equatorial counter-
current which forced Drake on a more northerly course
across the Pacific.

'On account of the currents which hindered him he
directed his course towards China before he reached the
latitude of one and a half deg. north [the latitude of the
Moluccas]. From there they went to the island of 'los
Ladrones' [or Thieves] in nine deg.' The crossing took
sixty-eight days, during which time no land was sighted.
He then turned south to make for the Moluccas and
presumably to avoid possible encounters with the
Spanish near the Philippines. On 30 September (the
'Anonymous Narrative' recorded 13 October) the ship
reached some islands in 8° or 9°N which have been
identified as the Palau Islands, in the Western Carolines.

This map of the Pacific Ocean was probably based on
the maps of the Spanish cosmographer and chronicler,

López de Velasco. A similar manuscript map by
Velasco, preserved in the John Carter Brown library,
which is entitled 'Demarcacion y division de las Indias'
ca 1580, shows not only Spanish claims to the
Portuguese East Indies but also the routes taken by the
galleons between Manila in the Philippines and
Acapulco in Mexico. Depending on the season of the
year, crossings were made in about 8°N from Acapulco
to the Phillipines. The eastward voyage from Manila to
Acapulco was made by sailing north to about 40°
latitude, where the prevailing northwest winds would
facilitate a quick passage to the Californian coast, and
thence south to Acapulco.

From the reluctant pilot Colchero, Drake probably
gleaned as much information as possible about the
prevailing winds and currents in the Pacific. He also
obtained a navigational chart probably based on the
chart drawn by Andrés de Urdaneta who had sailed
across the Pacific with Legazpi in 1564–5. Although a
copy of the map was found in Mexico and another at the
Biblioteca Nacional in Lima neither copy now survives.
The Lima map was destroyed by fire in 1943. The
continuing use of this chart is attested by one Juan de
Grijalva who wrote in 1592: 'arriving at the port of
Acapulca Father Urdaneta drew a chart with all its
winds and routes, points and capes so well that it is being
still followed today'. On the Herrera map, as on so many
Spanish maps, the extent of the Pacific is greatly under-
estimated (probably deliberately). The Moluccas are
shown only 110° west of Peru instead of the true 150°.

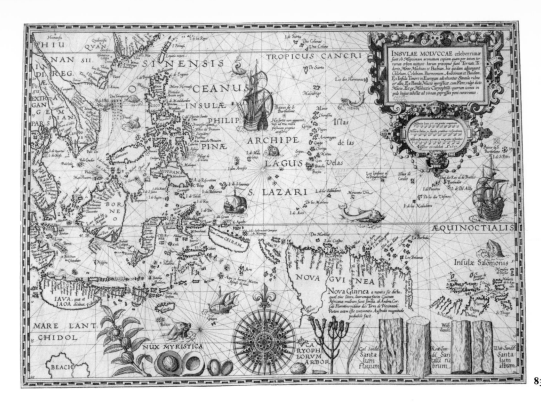

83 To the Moluccas

Insulae Moluccae celeberrimae . . .
C. J. Visscher excudebat A⁰. 1617.
41 × 58 cm   *Maps C.2.a.3.(4)*

At the Palau Islands, which Drake named the 'Island of Thieves' (on account of the natives' alleged propensity for pilfering) the ship's company was evidently amazed by the inhabitants' appearance; distended ear-lobes pierced with ornaments, finger nails an inch long and 'teeth as blacke as pitch'. About a hundred canoes came to greet the *Golden Hind* but, as John Drake later recorded, the natives came armed with spears and stones and seemed very warlike. In the event twenty of them were killed before the ship hurriedly departed for the south-east coast of Mindanao, some thirteen days away. After having taken water on board and persuaded two or three Indians aboard as pilots, the *Golden Hind* sailed south past the island of Talao (now Talaud?) in 3°40′N.

At some point Drake sighted and gave chase to a Portuguese vessel which was *en route* from Malacca to Tidore where the Portuguese had established themselves, but he failed to overhaul the ship. When the *Golden Hind* came in sight of Ternate, the most northerly of the Molucca Islands, Sultan Babu (Baber in the English accounts) sent two *caracoas* (see **84**) to the ship. On learning that Drake was no friend to the Portuguese, with whom Babu was in constant conflict, he invited Drake to anchor at Ternate rather than at

Tidore where the Portuguese had a 'galley and a galleon with which they could do much damage'.

This printed map engraved by Johannes à Doetechum for the Dutch scholar, Petrus Plancius in 1592–4, was based on the work of a Portuguese cartographer Bartolemeu Lasso. In a manuscript document dated 15–17 April 1592, the States General of the Netherlands made known that they had authorized by patent 'Cornelis Claesz printer in Amsterdam . . . to print or draw . . . such twenty five special sea charts as he obtained by the direction of Mr. Petrus Plancius, but at his own expense, from Bartholomeo de Lasso cosmographer to the King of Spain.' This chart was first published 1592–4 and revealed some of the prevailing misconceptions about the East Indies and south-west Pacific. The Palau Islands, then called the 'Isles de Sequiera', are not depicted and the island of Celebes does not bear its true shape (*c.f.* map III, p. 85); the east coast, along which Drake was to have so much difficulty, is erroneously rendered as an almost straight north to south line. The island of Talao (now Talaud?) is however marked immediately south of the island of 'Carangao' (Sarangan?).

On this, the third state of the map, the engraver's name has been erased and that of the publisher Claesz Johannes Visscher added together with the date 1617. At the bottom are shown the aromatic spices which composed the lucrative trade of the Moluccas; nutmeg (*nux mystica*), cloves (*caryophilorum arbor*) and various sandalwoods (*santalum*).

84 Sultan Babu greets Drake at Ternate

Carcoa, ou Corcorra du Roy de Ternate.
In: Bartoleme Argensola *Histoire de la Conquête des Isles Moluques*. Amsterdam, 1706. Vol. 1, p. 168.
16 × 20 cm   *146.a.25*

As ruler of Ternate, Sultan Babu controlled the islands of Motir and Maquian and thus the bulk of the clove trade. He had also just succeeded in ejecting the Portuguese from Ternate and was evidently pleased to meet the Englishmen. He arranged for four canoes to tow the *Golden Hind* into port on the east coast of the island, probably at Talangam where the old Portuguese fort stood. Babu then went to meet the *Golden Hind* in great state. 'The manner of his coming, as it was princely, so truly it seemed to us very strange and marvellous', recorded the compiler of *The World Encompassed*.

The royal *caracoa* was a large open canoe with a high prow and stern, with outrigger rowing galleys manned by about eighty slaves, two to an oar. On a raised platform above the canoe sat two men who beat out the timing of each paddle stroke on a tabor and on 'sounding basons of metal'. In the same place were mounted 'seven Brass Guns; a considerable number of Pikes advanc'd . . . and a bed adorn'd with Quilts interwoven with Gold.' The King sat or lay on 'that rich bed, the servants of his Bedchamber Fanning him with a large wing [*i.e.* fan] made of various colour'd feathers.' Babu promised to come on board the following day but sent his brother instead to invite Drake ashore. Although the account in *The World Encompassed* hinted that some friction had occurred between Drake and Babu, the compiler was content to record that the 'King's brother had uttered certaine words, in secret conference with our Generall aboard, his Cabbin, which bred no small suspicion of ill intent.' Drake was persuaded not to go ashore.

85 The Sultan entertains

Le Roy de Ternate Regale les Hollandois et leur Donne le Spectacle des Escrimeurs.
In: Bartoleme Argensola *Histoire de la Conquête des Isles Moluques*. Amsterdam, 1706. Vol. 3, p. 46.
16 × 20 cm   *146.a.25*

Drake sent a party of his men ashore however to visit the Sultan who greeted them at his court. A later illustration of a feast given in honour of the Dutch was included in the French edition of Bartolome Argensola's *Conquista de las Islas Malucas* published in 1706 which reveals something of the splendour of such an occasion. The Dutch were entertained with an exhibition of dancing by Moluccan warriors.

Drake's men were evidently sent as emissaries to the Sultan, although *The World Encompassed* does not reveal the nature of their business. They were amazed by

84

Babu's sumptuous attire: 'From the wast to the ground was all cloth of gold, and that very rich; his legges bare, but on his feet a paire of shooes of cordiuant, [*i.e.* leather] died red . . . about his necke hee had a chaine of perfect gold . . . [and] on his left hand was a Diamond, an Emerald, a Ruby and a Turky, [*i.e.* turquoise] 4 very faine and perfect jewells.'

86 The Clove Trade

Conquista de las Islas Malucas . . . Escrita por . . . Bartoleme Leonardo de Argensola Madrid, 1609.
29 cm   *983 f.20*

On the subjection of the Portuguese crown to Philip II in 1580, the governor of the Philippines, Gonzalo Ronquillo de Peñalosa, sent Francisco de Dueñas to investigate the political situation in the Moluccas. Whilst there Dueñas discovered that Francis Drake had established some sort of agreement with Sultan Babu at Ternate: in exchange for the clove trade English ships would protect Ternate from the Portuguese. Dueñas's manuscript report is now preserved in the archives at Seville and provides a more detailed and balanced account of Drake's activities than either *The World Encompassed* or John Drake's later depositions. The general veracity of the report is confirmed in part by a subsequent letter from Ronquillo to Philip II dated 25 June 1582, where he warned the King that if the English 'consider well the matter, they will think very highly of the Molucos which they can take and keep with a few forces.' Bartoleme Argensola in his history of the Moluccas described how Dueñas, disguised as a Chinaman, travelled about the islands in Chinese and Malay vessels assessing the islands' fortifications and armaments. When Argensola related Drake's activities in Ternate, however, he seems to have used some other source as well. He confirmed John Drake's brief story that Drake 'traded for cloves and ginger' and that 'the King wished to kill him'. Argensola explained this turn of events by saying that Drake 'attempted to barter for Clove without his leave [and] was informed how severely he [the Sultan] handled such as transgressed, and slighting this advice, the King came to hear of it, and ordered him [Drake] to be killed.' Drake then appeased the Sultan with presents which Dueñas lists as a gold ring set with a precious stone, a coat of mail and a very fine helmet.

The World Encompassed remains silent on this incident and on the subsequent arrangement; but evidently the Spanish and John Drake were convinced that Babu and Drake had entered into such an agreement. Argensola recorded that the Sultan gave Drake a 'rich Ring' for the Queen and that 'he [Drake] sailed homewards with a great quantity of clove'. The 'Anonymous Narrative' noted that six tons of cloves were loaded on board. In 1605 a later Sultan of Ternate wrote a letter to King James I, printed by Samuel Purchas, reminding him of Drake's earlier voyage and of the ring sent 'unto the Queene of England, as a token of remembrance between us'.

87

87 Crab Island

'Van den Cancer Crumenatus'
In: G. E. Rumphius, *D'Amboinsche Rariteitkamer*.
Amsterdam, 1705. pl. IV.
40 cm   *459.d.7*

After four or five days' stay at Ternate, Drake set sail to the south-west for a safer place to careen the ship and repair the decayed water casks. On 14 November the *Golden Hind* arrived at an island in 1°40′S which was thought to be to 'the south of Celebes'. The identification of the island, which was variously called 'Crab' Island, 'Francisca' Island and, by Dueñas, 'Coro' Island, has never been established. The difficulty of locating it is further complicated by Drake's ignorance (which he shared with his contemporaries) of the true shape of Celebes. With its three eastward peninsulas (see Map III, p. 85), it was completely at variance with the Portuguese charts available which showed an elongated island lying in latitudes 2°N to 5°S with only the most northerly peninsula, forming the gulf of Tomini, depicted (see **83**). Drake is generally assumed to have repaired his ship on one of the islands of the Banggai archipelago which lies in about 1°–2°S off Celebes.

On Crab Island the crew were amazed to observe the large edible crabs that abounded on land. These were described by Charles de l'Écluse in his notes on the voyage (see also **55, 89**) and are generally assumed to be identifiable with the robber crab (*cancer crumenatus*). L'Écluse recorded that in the dense woods of the island lived large numbers of these crustaceans which ate grass and lived in holes at the roots of trees. The starving men, after a few days, boiled and ate the crabs. They gained the impression that the crabs lived on land all the time, as when they threw the crabs into the sea they immediately scuttled back to dry land. Robber crabs can grow to a width of two feet and *The World Encompassed* (which called them crayfish) asserted that one crab was sufficient 'to satisfie foure hungry men at a dinner'.

There the ship stayed on the stocks for twenty-six days. A smith's forge was set up inside the fortified encampment 'both for the making of some necessarie ship-worke, and for the repairing of some iron-hooped caskes [*i.e.* water casks].' On 12 December the *Golden*

Hind, with a company of sixty men, left the island hoping to sail to the west round Celebes but the ship was soon forced south by the south-east trend of the coast and the prevailing north-east wind.

88 The 'Golden Hind' aground

Inset view of the *Golden Hind* aground entitled 'Lamentabla description du maniere du dit signeur drack eschoue et hurtant co[n]tre le rock . . .'
In: La Herdike [*i.e.* Heroike] Enterprinse faict par le signeur Draeck. [Antwerp?, *ca* 1583.]
Maps C.2.a.7.(1)

Trapped by the winds and the coast of Celebes, Drake made his way south through coastal shoals. On 8 or 9 January 1580 the *Golden Hind* ran aground upon a reef in about 2°S. Stuck fast, the ship heeled over and in order to save her, three tons of cloves, two cannon and a quantity of meal and beans were thrown overboard. Significantly perhaps neither gold nor silver was heaved over the side. In the hope of Divine intervention, Francis Fletcher, the preacher, gave a sermon and administered communion to the assembled company. The content of his sermon is not preserved but it was evidently of a recriminatory nature, for Drake, in a fit of temper, 'excomvnicated' Fletcher shortly after the ship was refloated. Presumably Fletcher had declared the disaster was in recompense for the piratical activities on the voyage, and no doubt mentioned Doughty's execution. Fletcher found himself chained to one of the hatches in the forecastle, while Drake sat 'with a peire of pantoffles in his hand' and declared to the company that

88

he denounced Fletcher 'to the divell and all his angells, and then hee chardged him uppon payne of death not once to come before the mast for if hee did he swore hee should bee hanged, and Drake cawsed a posy to bee written and bound about Fletcher's arme with chardge that if he tooke it of[f], hee should then bee hanged.' The text was 'Frances fletcher ye falsest knave that liveth.'

Drake's misfortune on the reef did not go unnoticed. Sultan Babu, according to Dueñas, ordered 'a certain bronze cannon of marvelous size' to be brought up from the bottom of the sea and he then 'built a house in front of his palace in order to put it on the roof in open view, mounted ready to fire.'

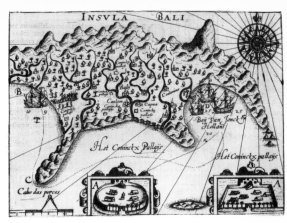

89 Barativa Island

Fructus Beretinus.
In: *Caroli Clusii Atreb. aliqvot notæ in Garciæ Aromatum Historiam.eiusdem descriptiones nonnullarum Stirpium, & aliarum exoticarum rerum, quæ à Generoso vir Francisco Drake . . . obseruatae sunt . . .* Antverpiae, 1582.
17 cm   *988.f.2.(2)*

On 20 January fierce westerly winds blew the *Golden Hind* to the east through the Banda Sea for over two weeks. Not until 8 February did the ship find an anchorage at the town of Baratina or Barativa on an island in 7°15′S. The island has been conjecturally identified as Damma (or Damar) lying to the north of Timor. On the island the English found a species of nut, specimens of which they took home. Charles de l'Écluse recounted in his notes on the botanical specimens found on the voyage that the nut was edible. The natives boiled it and, after beating it, cooked it as a kind of porridge. L'Écluse included a picture of the nut in his work and acknowledged the kindness of one Richard Garth of London, and of Dr Hugh Morgan, the Queen's physician, in communicating the information to him. Members of the ship's company also told him how they had previously found the fruit on an uninhabited island and although they were starving they had not dared to eat it.

The nut was probably a species of *Canarium*, probably the *Canarium vulgare* which is found in the Lesser Sunda Islands, Celebes and the Moluccas.

90 The island of Bali

Insula Bali.
In: Cornelis Houtman *Diarium Nauticum itineris Batavorum in Indiam Orientalem.* Amsterdam, 1598.
20 cm   *1486.gg.17*

The first Dutch expedition to the East Indies 1595–7, under Cornelis Houtman, gained the impression that the natives of Bali remembered the voyage of Francis Drake, 1577–80. Houtman's ship sailed from Bantam on the north coast of Java, where they had procured an agreement to trade in pepper, to the island of Bali. At the eastern end of the island in a bay which they called 'Parvæ Bataviæ' ('Baij van Jonck Hollant') the inhabitants recalled that some eighteen or nineteen years previously 'a ship had anchored in that same place with people who were in some respects like us [i.e. the Dutch]. Amongst them were some who knew how to divide a rope into five or six parts and then make the rope whole again.' A reference perhaps to the art of splicing rope which had evidently caught the natives' imagination.

In March 1588 Thomas Cavendish had passed through the Bali Channel between Java and Bali and it seems possible the islanders were remembering this visit rather than Drake's, although they specified eighteen or nineteen years as the period which had elapsed.

The account in *The World Encompassed* compresses a voyage of twenty-seven days from Barativa or Baratina island to south west Java (possibly the port of Tjilatjap) into a few lines, identifying none of the islands which were passed. It does however seem to indicate that Drake passed to the south of the Sawoe Islands in '10° and some odd minutes', and that after this he 'past on to the Westward without stay or anything to be taken notice of till 9 March when in the morning we espied land . . . in 8°20′S . . . This Iland we found to be the Iland Java.'

91 The South Coast of Java

Java. De Kleine Baai Srigonjo Zuidk. v. Java.
In: *Java. Naar Schilderijen en Teekenningen van A. Salm . . . Opsteen gebracht door J. C. Greive, Jr.* Amsterdam, [1876] pl. 6.
46 × 63 cm   *Maps 143.e.17*

One of twenty-four coloured lithographed views of the island of Java, this plate shows the Bay of Srigonjo on the south coast in the province of Malang. In 1580 the south coast of Java had not been explored; nor was it depicted on any current Portuguese charts, although the island was in regular receipt of Portuguese ships along its northern coast. The Portuguese were presumably well aware, since the island's first depiction in the rutter drawn by the pilot, Francisco Rodrigues, about 1513, that the south coast existed. Francis Drake sailed along the south coast of the island, out of sight of land, for about a week before reaching a port which has been identified as Tjilatjap.

92   The Port of Java

Hydrographische Kaart van het Zeegat van
Tjilatjap, Opgenomen door den Luitenant ter zee,
P. J. B. De Perez . . . 1839 . . . uitgegeven door
Jacob Swart. Te Amsterdam bij de Wed. Gerard
Hulst van Keulen 1847 [Verbeterd in 1858].
56 × 73 cm   *Maps 89060(2)*

There is only one harbour of any significance on the south coast of Java, Tjilatjap, which lies in the middle of the island's coastline at latitude 7°45′S. *The World Encompassed* described the latitude of the middle of Java as 7°30′S, presumably from observations taken on shore at or near Tjilatjap. The Hondius broadside map (see **78**), which showed Drake's voyage round the world, included an inset of 'Portus Javæ Maioris' where Drake anchored and reprovisioned, which is here illustrated. The presence of a narrow inlet or canal, as shown on the inset, is indeed characteristic of the easterly approach to the port. On the south side of the Tjilatjap inlet is the rocky island of Noesa Kambangan, while to the north lies a spit of sand and the Tjilatjap promontory.

At the Javan port Drake entertained the native princes with a tour of his ship and accompanying music. The hospitality of the princes was overwhelming. Linens and silks (presumably da Silva's) were exchanged for hens,

rice, a whole ox and countless fruits including *sago*. Thomas Hood later noted, for Captain Edward Fenton's benefit, that Drake had exchanged goods to the value of about £4,000 in Java. The company stayed in harbour until 26 March when the ship set sail, re-trimmed and careened, for the Cape of Good Hope. The *Famous Voyage* recorded that the Javans had warned Drake that 'not farre off were such great ships as [the English]' which information probably expedited his departure.

This chart was published by Jacob Swart, one of the successors to the Dutch firm of Van Keulen which, since the mid-seventeenth century, had been printing charts of areas of commercial interest to the Dutch. The old firm's name was retained until 1885 when chart production passed to the Dutch Hydrographic Office.

93   An oyster tree at Sierra Leone

The Bamboo palm and the Mangrove or 'oyster tree' at Sierra Leone, drawn by Richard Madox.
In: The journal written by Richard Madox, chaplain, on a voyage to Brazil 1582–3, f. 36.
MS pen and ink sketch on paper.
23 cm   *Cotton MS Appendix XLVII.*

On 18 June the *Golden Hind* cleared the Cape of Good Hope and, having failed to find water in a bay on its west coast, put out to sea for Sierra Leone. The crew would surely have perished had not 'vi or vii toon of rayne water' replenished the water casks before the ship reached harbour. At the Cape, John Drake had noted that for the fifty-nine men on board, there were only three pipes of water and half a pipe of wine. On 22 July 1580 the ship anchored off Sierra Leone and the crew observed during their stay the strange behaviour of the 'tree oyster'. As described in the *Famous Voyage*, the 'Oisters [were] upon trees of one kinde, spawning and increasing infinitely, the Oisters suffering no bud to grow'. Richard Madox, Fellow of All Souls and chaplain to Edward Fenton's abortive expedition to the Moluccas in 1582–3, saw the same sight and recorded this view of oysters living on the coastal mangrove (*Rhizophora sp.*).

On 26 September 1580 the *Golden Hind* reached Plymouth, having taken '2 yeares 10 moneths and some odde few daies beside'.

94   The earliest printed discourse on the voyage

*A Discourse in commendation of the valiant as
vertuous minded Gentleman, Maister Frauncis
Drake, with a reioysing of his happy adventures.
Written by N. Breton, Gentleman.* At London,
Printed by John Charlewood, 1581. Eight leaves.
14 cm   *Lent by Hans P. Kraus*

Evidently written and published before Drake's

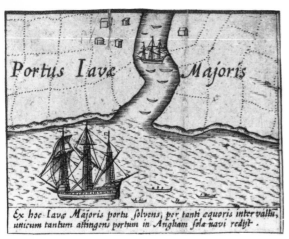

Ex hoc Iavæ Majoris portu solvens, per tanti æquoris intervalli, unicum tantum attingens portum in Angliam sola navi redijt.

92

knighting in 14 April 1581, this short, eulogistic celebration of Drake's voyage round the world was composed by the Elizabethan poet and writer, Nicholas Breton (*ca* 1545–*ca* 1622).

In the work Breton mentions the success of 'Our Countrey man [who] hath gone rounde about the whole world', and found 'the Lande where Treasure lies, the way to come by it and ye honor by the getting of it'. Evidently sensitive to Spanish charges of plunder in South America, Breton wisely omits the name of the 'Lande' in question.

95 The first narrative account of the voyage 1589

'The famous voyage of Sir Francis Drake into the South Sea and there hence about the whole Globe of the Earth.' Six unnumbered leaves between pp. 643–4 in Richard Hakluyt *The Principall Navigations, Voiages and Discoveries of the English Nation, made by Sea or over Land* . . . London, George Bishop and Ralph Newberie, 1589.
29 cm   *C.32.m.10*

The Principall Navigations was evidently almost ready for publication when Hakluyt decided to include an account of Sir Francis Drake's circumnavigation. In the preface to the reader Hakluyt explained that he had originally intended to insert an account of Sir Francis Drake's voyage, and had taken 'more then [than] ordinarie paines meaning to have inserted it in this worke'. He then recorded that he had been 'contray to my expectations, seriously delt withall, not to anticipate or prevent another mans paines and charge in drawing all the services of that worthy Knight into one volume.' The projected work did not materialize and the identity of the author who had undertaken to complete a biography of Drake remains unknown. John Stow had certainly collected a great deal of information about Drake's voyage, and amongst his surviving papers are to be found the manuscript sources of Hakluyt's detailed account. Perhaps Stow had intended to write more than his own note on the voyage which was included in the 1592 edition of his *Chronicles*. Whatever the case, Hakluyt decided to add six unnumbered leaves of text, giving the first detailed account of the voyage, to his *Principall Navigations*. Printed from the same batch of paper and from the same type as the rest of the book, these pages were inserted in as many copies as possible.

The voyage was based on two main identifiable sources: John Cooke's narrative (Harley MS 540. ff. 93ʳ–110ᵛ) and, for the second part of the voyage, the 'anonymous' journal (Harley MS 280. ff. 83–90). Although both manuscripts contain derogatory accounts of Drake's behaviour, Hakluyt evidently thought it best either to excise them entirely, or to put a more favourable construction on the events in question.

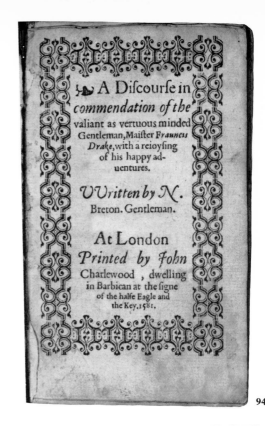

94

95

96a

96b

Presumably he also had access to Fletcher's manuscript, as some parts of his account resemble most closely the narrative of *The World Encompassed* (1628) which purported to rely heavily on Fletcher's journal.

Hakluyt's view of Drake's famous voyage, while not entirely uncritical of his personal conduct, was justly admiring and congratulatory. The success of the voyage offered, by way of example to other enterprising Englishmen, the chance to break the Spanish monopoly of trade and colonization as well the hope of plunder. As a promoter of numerous colonizing projects Hakluyt could readily appreciate Drake's achievement.

96 The commemorative silver medal

a   World map in two hemispheres, engraved or stuck
on silver, bearing the track of Drake's voyage
round the world, 1577–80.
Silver medal, diam. 68 mm
Lent by the B.M. Department of Coins & Medals
1882.5.7.1

b   A circular map of the eastern hemisphere showing
the track of part of Drake's circumnavigation from
the Moluccas to England, 1579–80.
On paper, diam. 68 mm
Harley 5957 (Bagford collection no. 19)

In the collection of 'the shoemaker and biblioclast' John Bagford (1650–1716), now preserved in the Department of Printed Books, a unique paper impression of the silver medal map was recently discovered. Showing the eastern hemisphere only, the paper impression exhibits not only the *intaglio* lines of the medal map exactly, but also the various accidental imperfections in the surface

of this copy of the medal. Within the Antarctic circle, for example, a number of minute 'black spots' may be seen which are to be found in the same positions on the medal. Similarly the outline of the tab (4 mm wide) on the north rim of the medal can be identified on the paper impression.

This paper map is presumably therefore a counter impression taken from this particular copy of the medal. The process by which such impressions could be made was well known to medallists. Briefly, a reversed impression of the medal was pulled from the inked surface of the silver, as from a copper plate. Before the ink could dry this reversed image on paper was passed through a press with a second piece of paper so that an impression the same way round as the engraved medal could be printed.

Presumably the earliest of the medals to be issued was that made and signed by Michael Mercator, *ca* 1589 (see **74**).

97 The 'Famous Voyage' on a map

La Herdike [*i.e.* Heroike] Enterprinse faict par le
signeur Draeck d'avoir cirquit toute la terre.
Nicola van Sype f.
[Antwerp?, *ca* 1583.]
24 × 44 cm   *Maps C.2.a.7.(1)*

Probably the earliest of the engraved maps recording Drake's circumnavigation, this map exhibits some of the features of the large map presented by Sir Francis Drake to Queen Elizabeth in October 1580 (see **99**). Purporting to have been seen and corrected by Drake, ('veuee et corige par le dict siegneur drach') the map shows the

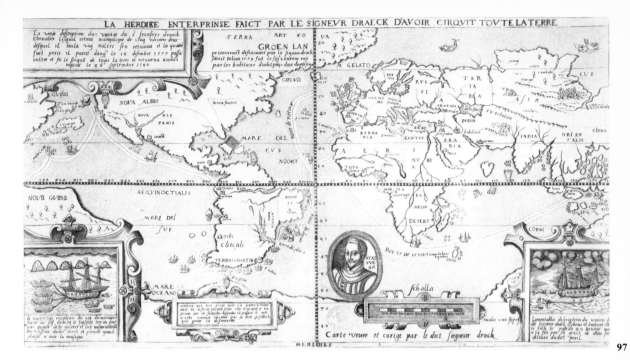

route of Drake's voyage with some accuracy.

To the south of Tierra del Fuego lay the islands which Drake had discovered and, in particular, Elizabeth Island which Drake claimed for England. Both this island and 'Nova Albion' are shown with the Royal Arms of England. Similarly both the Queen's map and this engraved version included a legend (one in Latin, the other in French) explaining that the land to the south of the Magellan Strait was not *Terra Firma* as previously believed but a series of islands and channels. In the East Indies, Java is clearly shown as an island with the route of the *Golden Hind* marked, passing along the south coast and stopping at a port, probably Tjilatjap (see **92**). Also included on the map is an oval portrait of Drake aged forty-two years, which, assuming his birth to have occurred in 1540–1, indicates a date of 1582–3 or later for the completion of the design for this map or perhaps for its engraving. A number of contemporary portraits

survive, including the miniature painted by Nicholas Hilliard in 1581, on which this inset portrait may well be based.

Nothing is known about the engraver 'Nicola van Sype', although a family of engravers of the same name was at work in Germany in the first two decades of the seventeenth century. A Dutch text version of the map is also known which is generally considered to have been copied from this French edition.

Queen Elizabeth was not the only person to receive a manuscript map of Drake's voyage. Edmund Grindal (1519?–1583), Archbishop of Canterbury from 1576 to 1583, is said to have received one. More interestingly perhaps Henri IV of France wrote to Walsingham on 12 March 1585 requesting a copy and a richly decorated example (*diapré et doré*) was sent to Paris (noted in B.N. Manuscrit français 15454 f. 133). No example of the map is now known to survive.

IX

Drake's reception in England

IN October 1580 Drake was summoned to court by Queen Elizabeth, where he enthralled her for six hours with his traveller's tales. His presence, however, posed certain problems for the Queen. What was to be done with the booty? Was Drake to be prosecuted for piracy, like John Wynter, and for murder as Thomas Doughty's brother desired? The Spanish ambassador Bernardino de Mendoza immediately demanded restitution of the Spanish treasure, and his letters to Philip II (now mainly preserved in the archives at Simancas) provide a valuable commentary on Drake's return, lacking in English sources. Elizabeth made it plain she was in no mood to give up the treasure, although eventually some of the bullion was restored via the dubious agency of one Peter Zubiaur. Drake was discreetly given £10,000 from the plunder before it was removed from the *Golden Hind* at Plymouth, whence it was taken to Saltash Castle, registered, and then carried to Sion House on its way to the safety of the Tower of London. Having supervised the treasure's removal Drake returned to court and was much in the Queen's favour.

On New Year's Day, the day on which English monarchs traditionally received gifts, the Queen wore a crown made from emeralds from Peru that Drake had given her. The Spanish ambassador said it had five emeralds set in it, three of them almost as long as a little finger whilst the two round ones were valued at 20,000 crowns; Drake gave her other gifts too. The Queen ordered the *Golden Hind* to be brought to Deptford for all London to see. Drake entertained her on board ship with a banquet on 4 April 1581. Mendoza said the banquet was 'finer than has ever been seen in England since the time of King Henry'; the Queen told Drake she had brought a gilded sword to cut off his head but instead she handed the sword to Monsieur de Marchaumont, a French envoy sent to prepare the way for the Duc d'Alençon, brother of the King of France and a suitor for Elizabeth's hand, telling him she authorized him to perform the ceremony of knighting Drake for her, thus associating France in an action that was calculated to inflame the King of Spain and his ambassador.

The Queen commanded the *Golden Hind* to be preserved at Deptford as a perpetual memory of Drake's voyage. The vessel became one of the sights of London though soon after Drake's death it began to fall into disrepair. A chair made from its timbers (**III**) was given in 1662 to the Bodleian Library, Oxford.

Hilliard's miniature of Drake is dated 1581 and it must have been about this time, as a result of

Drake's fame, that the Hondius engraving was made. Drake bought Buckland Abbey, near Plymouth, with some of the spoils of his voyage. He was mayor of Plymouth in 1581–2 and in January 1582 the Queen conferred on him the manor of Sherford, near Kingsbridge in Devon. His first wife died and was buried on 25 January 1583 at St Budeaux, in the church where they had been married. He remarried in 1585, his second wife being Elizabeth Sydenham, the heiress of Sir George Sydenham of Coombe Sydenham in Somerset. He became Member of Parliament for Bossiney in North Cornwall in 1584 and sat in several Parliaments.

100b

98 John Wynter acquitted of piracy

A declaration of acquittal of charges of piracy dated 6 April 1582.
MS 19 × 24 cm

*Lent by Mr J. R. W. Blathwayt
(deposited in the Gloucestershire County
Record Office D 1799 T3)*

By June 1580, before Drake's return, the Portuguese ambassador, Don Antonio de Castillo, had evidently sought restitution of the goods seized in Nuño da Silva's ship at Santiago and brought back by John Wynter in the *Elizabeth*. Little remained but a few pieces of canvas and some linens. John Wynter was called to give evidence before the High Court of Admiralty and, as is shown by this document, he was 'acquicted and discharged from all mysdeameanures of pyracyes w^ch . . . was supposed against him by the Portingalles that had bynne comytted in the tyme while the saide John Wynter was upon the Seas in companie wth Francis Drake.' The declaration is signed by Anne Wynter (wife of George Wynter deceased), Sir William Wynter, David Lewes, judge of the Admiralty, John Popham, Her Majesty's Attorney-General, also Thomas Ivye and Thomas Hamam the executors of George Wynter's will.

99 The Queen greets Francis Drake

Bernardino de Mendoza, the Spanish ambassador in London, to Philip II, King of Spain, 16 October 1580. *Spanish.*
30 × 21 cm   *Additional MS 28420, f.30*

Mendoza reports that Drake has been summoned to Court by the Queen and has spent more than six hours ('*mas de seis horas*') with her. Moreover, advised by Sir Christopher Hatton, Walsingham, Leicester, and others, the Queen has ordered a rumour to be put about that Drake has not brought much money back from his travels.

Drake gave Elizabeth a journal of everything that had happened during the three years he had been away and a large map. This map is presumably that described by the chronicler, Samuel Purchas, as hanging in James I's 'Gallerie at White Hall, neere the Privie Chamber'. He further describes the chart as follows: 'In which Map, the South of the Magelane Straits is not a Continent, but many Ilands . . . The Name Elizabeth is expressed in golden letters, with a golden Crowne, Garter, and Armes affixed: The words ascribed thereunto are these, *Cum omnes ferè hanc partem Australem Continentem esse putent, pro certo sciant Insulas esse Navigantibus peruias, earumque australissimam Elizabetham à D. Francisco Draco Inuentore dictam esse.*' (*Purchas His Pilgrimes* III, iii, 461.) A number of maps, presumably based on this chart, were later drawn and engraved (see **75, 78, 97**).

100 The Treasure

a Queen Elizabeth to Edmund Tremayne, Richmond 24 October 1580.
MS 31 × 23 cm

Lent by the P.R.O.; SP 12/143 no. 30

Edmund Tremayne (*d.* 1582) of Collacombe, Lamerton, Devonshire, was a Clerk of the Privy Council. The Queen wrote to him instructing him to assist Drake in sending to London the bullion taken during the voyage. It was to be registered, a necessary formality if restitution was to be made, but here the Queen tells Tremayne, *sub rosa*, to give Drake £10,000 worth of bullion before the registration begins.

b List of ingots in the Tower, 24 December 1580. Signed by Alderman Richard Martyn, Christopher Harris and Francis Drake.
MS 31 × 20 cm

Lent by the P.R.O.; SP12/144 no. 60.

Early in December 1580 the bullion was brought to the Tower, 'laid up in a vaute under ye Jewellhouse', and weighed. The amount registered is colossal and certainly justified the Spanish Ambassador's indignation. The register of the treasure shows that there was 22,899lb 5oz, that is to say over ten tons of silver bullion, 512lb 6oz of coarse silver and 101lb 10oz of gold bullion. The final sheet of the register with the gold bullion total, here exhibited, was signed as correct on

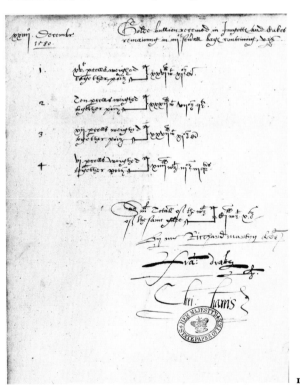

Elizabeth R

Trustie and wellbeloved we greet you well. Whereas
by letters lately written unto you by our commande-
ment from Sir Francis Walsyngham you were
willed in our name to yelde your assistaunce
unto our wellbeloved subiect Francis Drake
for the sone bestowing of certen bullyon lately
by him brought into this our realme, wch our
pleasure is shold now be sent up as you shall
further understand by the said Drake, wherin
you are to assist him according to soch direction as you shall receyve from our privie
counsell: These are therfor to let you under-
stande yt we are pleased for certen good consi-
derations that ther shold be left in the handes
of the said Drake so myche of the said bullyon
by him brought home as may amount unto
the somme of ten thousand poundes, wch we
requyre you to be performed accordingly
and forasmuch for sundrye good respectes
we thinke yt very meet that the leaving
of the said somme in his handes to your self
be kept most secreat, we therfor charge you that
the same be kept accordingly, wherof we need
not to dowbt having heretofore by former ac-
quentaunce had so good profe of your secrecie.
Geven at our mannor of Richmond the
xxvjth of October in the xxvijth yeare of our
reigne.

102 Detail: some of the signatures of Drake's crew.

24 December 1580 by Christopher Harris, in whom Edmund Tremayne had expressed his confidence to Walsingham in November 1580, saying that he had long treated him as a son; by Richard Martin (1534–1617) an alderman (later sheriff and Lord Mayor of the City of London, also a goldsmith and Warden of the Mint); and by Francis Drake.

101 Charges against Drake

'The Answer of the Span. Ambassadour.'
MS 31 × 18 cm   *P.R.O. S.P.94/1/57a*

On 23 October two secretaries of the Council, namely Beale and Wilkes, were sent to see Mendoza. Through these emissaries, the Queen informed Mendoza that she understood he was complaining about Drake's depredations of Spanish subjects in South America, and that he had no right to do so until she received a

satisfactory account of Spanish activities in Ireland. By way of reply Mendoza listed Spanish grievances, the principal charge being that: 'The spoile is of great importance: a great quantity of bullion: and pearles taken in Mare del Sur, appertaining partly unto the King, and partly unto his Subjects.' Mendoza then cited the case of piracy against John Wynter to establish Drake's known piratical proclivities: 'And young Wenters [Wynter's] report of his spoiles don uppon the Portingales in his going out, the Interest and Right whereof is now come to the King his M^r [*i.e.* Philip II], is sufficient to prove His Piracy, and to demand Justice.'

102 Drake's crew answer the charges

The answer of forty-nine members of Drake's company to questions concerning the circumnavigation and their conduct during the voyage, enclosed in a letter written by Edmund Tremayne to Sir Francis Walsingham, 8 November 1580.
MS 31 × 23 cm   *P.R.O. S.P.12/144 no. 17ii*

Requested to assist Drake refute Mendoza's charges, Edmund Tremayne questioned the ship's company, which remained in Plymouth, about the value of the bullion taken. He inquired whether they had seized any Spanish or Portuguese ships and had subsequently sunk them, and whether they had, 'at any tyme in any fight killed any of the said Ks subjects or had cut off their hands or armes or otherwise wth any crueltie mangled any of them.' To these points Lawrence Eliot, John Chester, Gregory Cary and George Fortescue replied that they knew some gold and silver had been taken 'but a verie small some in respect of that, that is reported.' Although ships had been seized none had been sunk. As to injuries received by the Spanish, Eliot recalled that 'only on[e] man I remember was hurt in the face, wch o^r General cawsed to be sent for, and lodged him in his owne shipp, seet him at his own table, and would not soffer him to depart before he was recovered.' Beneath the replies were the names of forty-five more crew members. All the names in the second column and some in the third column appear to be signed in the same hand. Tremayne evidently considered the replies truthful for he ended his letter 'By wch yo maie sone see how much things be infered beyonde the truth'.

103 Prosecuted for murder

'The confessyons of Pattrike Mays[o]n beinge compelled unto the same the [blank] daye of Maye 1582.'
MS 30 × 24 cm   *P.R.O. S.P.12/153 no. 49*

On the return of the *Golden Hind*, John Doughty, the surviving Doughty brother, attempted to take his legal revenge on Francis Drake. He himself had been kept under some sort of 'house arrest' on board during the course of the voyage, for Francisco Zarate had recalled that Doughty had not been allowed to go ashore at Guatulco: 'They do not do this to guard me but rather I think they did it to guard him'.

Once in England, John Doughty pressed his case in the Earl Marshal's court, the High Court of Chivalry and Honour. It seems quite likely that Drake managed to delay proceedings by questioning whether the Court had jurisdiction over matters 'beyond the Sea'. Chief Justice Wray ruled that the Court did have such competence. In the event however, a point of law prevented the case from being heard. The Court's ability to try cases 'of things done out of the realm' necessitated the presence not only of the Earl Marshal but also the Chief Constable. In 1581 there was no such officer. The Queen refused to grant a petition 'by the Heir to make a Constable', as is later recorded by the lawyers, Sir Edward Coke and Sir Richard Hutton. At that, the appeal or case 'slept'. (*Sed regina noluit constituere constabularium Angliae &c. et ideo dormivit appellum.*)

The conflict between John Doughty and Drake did not rest there. In May 1582, one Patrick Mason confessed under torture that John Doughty was implicated in a plot to kidnap or murder Drake. Mason claimed that Peter Zubiaur (the Spanish agent responsible for recovering Spanish losses sustained on Drake's voyage) had shown him letters from Spain, 'how the Kinge of Spaine have made prolemacon [proclamation] that whosoever woulde take upon him to conveye Sr Francis Drake out of this realme or to presente his heade unto him he shoulde have for his paines twentie thowsande ducketts.' Mason was told to persuade John Doughty to perform the deed. As a result of this revelation and information supplied by Francis Drake of Doughty's 'speeches uttered against him on his being knighted', John Doughty was committed to the Marshalsea. There he remained until 27 October 1583 when he petitioned that he might be tried or released. He was not however released and his ultimate fate is not known.

104 The Knighting

The Annales, or Generall Chronicle of England, begun first by maister Iohn Stow and after him continued and augmented with matters forreyne and domestique . . . vnto the end of this present yeere 1614 by Edmond Howes. Londini Impensis Thomae Adams, 1615, p. 807.
33 cm   *L.7.g.11*

Edmond Howes, in his 1615 continuation of the *Annales* (1580) of John Stow (1525?–1605), wrote that the news of Drake's great wealth 'so far fetcht was marvelous strange, and of all men held impossible, and incredible, but both prouing true, it fortuned, that many misliked

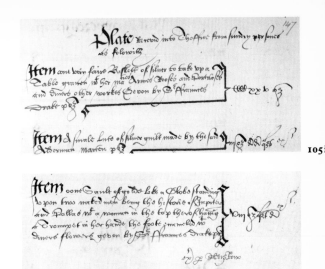

105i

105ii

it'; however, on 4 April 1581
'the Queenes Maiesty came aboorde his weather beaten Barke: where beeing as highly graced as his heart coulde wish, with knightly honour, Princely commendations and encouragement: forthwith visited his freinds in Courte, Towne, and Countrey, his name and fame became admirable in all places . . .'.
Camden said that as the Queen
'honoured Drake with the dignity of Knighthood . . . a slight Bridge made of Boords, by which people went into the Ship was broken downe by the Multitude, and about a hundred persons fell with it; they neuertheless received no harme at all: in somuch, that the Ship seemed to haue been built in a happy coniunction of the Planets.'

105 Drake's presents for the Queen

'Item oone very faire Baskett of siluer to take up a Table grauen with her Maties Armes Rooses and Portcloses and diuers other workes . . .'
40 cm   *Stowe MS 555, f.147*

This gift is probably the large coffer which Mendoza said Drake gave to the Queen on the occasion of his knighting. It is recorded by the staff of the Queen's Jewel-house in this manuscript as a 'Baskett' for clearing the table. It was probably a 'voider', that is to say, a tray, basket or other vessel in which dirty dishes or utensils, fragments of broken food etc., are placed whilst clearing a table during a meal.

A second gift by Drake to the Queen is recorded later in this same volume (f. 149, also illustrated) namely, 'oone Sault of golde like a Globe'. This globe salt was decorated with green enamel, representing the seas.

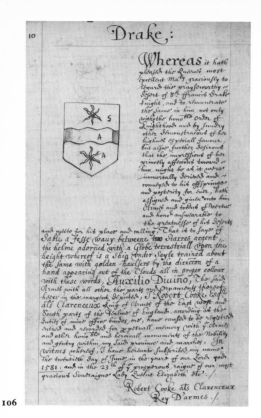

106

106 Drake's arms

Robert Cooke, Clarenceux King of Arms, records the grant of arms to Drake, 20 June 1581; *transcript* early seventeenth century.
32 cm   *Harley MS 1172, f.5b*

Having knighted Drake in April 1581, the Queen '. . . assigned . . . unto him Armes and tokens of Vertue . . . of Sable a fesse wauy betweene two Starres argent the helme adorned with a Globe terrestriall upon the height whereof is a Ship vnder Sayle trained about the same with golden haulsers by the direccon of a hand appearing out of the Clouds all in proper collour with these words, Auxilio Diuino.' All that appears in the unfinished sketch of the arms in this manuscript is the shield.

107 Francis Drake

Miniature of Sir Francis Drake by Nicholas Hilliard, 1581.
On vellum. Circular, diam. 2.9 cm
                    Lent by the National Portrait Gallery 4851

A fine portrait of Drake by the Court miniaturist, Nicholas Hilliard (1547–1619). Dr Auerbach considered it an authentic likeness. A larger oval version of the same miniature is in the Kunsthistorisches Museum, Vienna.

Edmund Howes wrote in 1615 that 'Bookes, pictures, and ballades were published' in Drake's 'prayse' after the Queen had knighted him in April 1581.

The miniature was purchased from the collection of the Earl of Derby at Christie's on 8 June 1971 (lot 76), and is further described as number 44 in the 'Catalogue' in Erna Auerbach's *Nicholas Hilliard* (1961).

108 Elizabeth I

An oval miniature of Elizabeth I by Nicholas Hilliard. In a mount probably dating from the seventeenth century.
4.5 × 4 cm *Lent by the Victoria and Albert Museum*

Hilliard painted this portrait of the Queen in about 1585–90. The miniature was formerly in the English Royal Collection. James II took it with him in his flight to France in 1688 and it passed into Louis XIV's collection. At the time of the French Revolution it was brought back to England. It was bequeathed by its most recent owner, Mrs Doris Herschorn, to the Victoria and Albert Museum. The miniature is further described as number 83 in the 'Catalogue' in Auerbach's *Nicholas Hilliard* (1961).

107

109 Buckland

The East view of Buckland Priory in the County of Devon. Samuel & Nathaniel Buck delin. et sculp. Saltash, 1734.
25 × 43 cm
K. Top. XI. 108

Through the agency of his friends, Christopher Harris and John Hele, Drake used some of the proceeds from his voyage to buy himself a former Cistercian Abbey, Buckland Priory near Plymouth, for £3,400 from Sir Richard Grenville. Here his descendants remained until the house became National Trust property in 1951.

110 The Queen grants him Sherford Manor

Warrant for the grant of the Manor of Sherford to Francis Drake, 12 January 1582. *Latin.*
MS 31 × 57 cm
Lent by the P.R.O.; Warrants for the Great Seal Series II (c.82) bundle 1380.

Warrant for the grant of the manor of Sherford in the county of Devon, with the reversion to certain other properties, to Francis Drake, knight, and his heirs. 'Given under our privy seal at our Palace of Westminster the twelfth day of January in the twenty fourth year of our reign.' The warrant states that the grant is made in recognition of the great honour Drake has brought to this kingdom by his journey round the globe from the west to the east, and by discovering and traversing many

parts of the southern world (*Australi mundi*) hitherto unknown.

In fact the manor of Sherford, which had once belonged to the priory of Plympton, was at this time leased to Drake's kinsmen, the Maynards, who continued to live there for many years.

THE EAST VIEW OF BUCKLAND PRIORY, IN THE COUNTY OF DEVON.

To Sir Francis Henry Drake Bart Proprietor of these Remains This Prospect is most gratefully inscribd by his much Oblig'd & very humble Servt Sams & Nath Buck

109

110

111

111 The 'Golden Hind' chair

An oak chair made from the timbers of the
Golden Hind ca 1662.
Lent by the Bodleian Library, Oxford

This chair, made from the timbers of Sir Francis
Drake's ship when it was broken up, was presented to
the Bodleian Library in 1662 by John Davies of
Camberwell, Keeper of naval stores at Deptford
dockyard. A plate fastened to the top of the chair records
this in the following words:

*Sella Ex Reliquijs tabulatorum Navis Dracanae
Fabricata Et a Joanne Davisio Depfordiensi
Arm : Navalium armamentorum Custode Regio
Bibliothecae Oxoniensi dedicata 1662.*

Attached to the back of the chair is a tablet bearing
commemorative verses in Latin by Abraham Cowley
which freely translated read:

To this great Ship which round the Globe has run,
And matcht in Race the Chariot of the Sun,
This Pythagorean Ship (for it may claime
Without Presumption so deserv'd a Name,
By knowledge once, and transformation now)
In her new shape, this sacred Port allow.
Drake & his Ship, could not have wisht from Fate
A more blest Station, or more blest Estate.
For Lo! a Seate of endles Rest is giv'n
To her in Oxford, and to him in Heav'n.

At least three other similar chairs are known to exist.
Cowley composed another poem about the chair which
he called an 'Ode. Sitting and Drinking in the Chair
made out of the Reliques of Sir Francis Drake's Ship.'

X

A privateering war in the West Indies 1585–6.

'THE damage this corsair did this city [*i.e.* Cartagena] amounts to more than 400,000 ducats, including the artillery which he carried off. He burned and demolished 248 houses, two-thirds of them masonry and tile, and one-third of them palmboard and thatch . . .' Thus the Spanish colonists bemoaned Drake's raid on the most important city in the Spanish main; a complaint echoed at Santiago in the Cape Verde Islands, Santo Domingo and San Augustin in Florida.

Drake's privateering raid was sponsored by a powerful assortment of London merchants and courtiers. It was probably envisaged by the Queen as a means of demonstrating England's sea power in a period of rapidly deteriorating relations between Spain and England. She also appreciated, as did the other promoters, the potential profits of Drake's enterprise. In all some twenty-two ships were ventured together with 2,300 men, including twelve companies of soldiers under the competent command of Lieutenant-General Christopher Carleill (*d.* 1593). Drake sailed on the *Elizabeth Bonaventure*, one of two Royal ships contributed.

The principal objective of the raid seems to have been plunder, as one of the Spanish colonists aptly remarked: 'For the principal purpose of this corsair is to prevent Your Majesty and private persons from receiving revenues from these parts.' In the planned itinerary of the voyage (**113**) it seems, however, that Drake and his captains also considered taking the town of Panama which controlled the bullion route from Peru across the isthmus to Nombre de Dios. They also proposed to destroy Havana in Cuba where both bullion fleets made rendezvous before setting sail for Seville (see p. 28). A permanent English presence in the West Indies as suggested by the more enthusiastic backers was not seriously considered. In the event, probably because of sickness in the fleet, Drake decided to make his way home without sacking Havana. He decided instead to relieve the colonists led by Ralph Lane at the Roanoke colony in Virginia which had been established by Walter Raleigh in 1585.

The fleet reached Portsmouth on 28 July 1586. Some 750 men had been lost on the voyage, many through disease, including Captain Walter Bigges whose narrative of the voyage is the main source for its history (**115**). Financially the expedition probably gave the adventurers a modest return of about fifteen shillings in the pound.

Although Drake's campaign left a harrowing impression on the Spanish colonists, the amounts of bullion reaching Spain did not decline, rather they increased. Philip II's war potential was not lessened and political tensions in Europe worsened. The final rupture between England and Spain became inevitable.

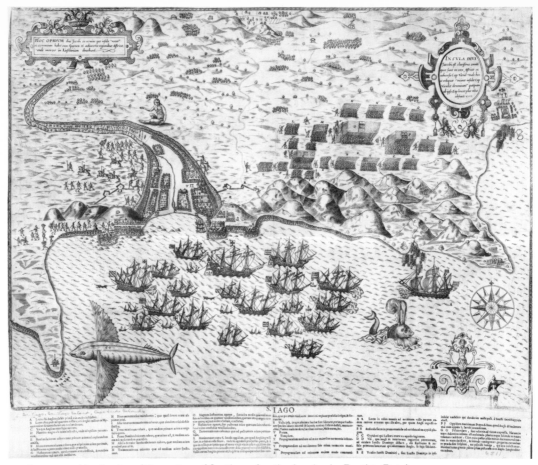

112 The 'Primrose' journal

> 'The discourse and description of the voyage of
> Sir Francis Drake and Mr. Captain Frobiser set
> forward the 14th day of September, 1585.'
> 32 cm   *Royal MS 7, CXVI, ff. 166–73a*

On 14 September 1585 a privateering fleet set sail under
Drake's command from Plymouth for the West Indies.
Sailing as his vice-admiral on the voyage was Martin
Frobisher who commanded the *Primrose*, a London
merchantman of 200 tons. At the last minute the Queen
hesitated to release the ships and to avoid a possible
countermanding order 'for we [were] not the most
assured of her Majesty's perseverance to let us go
forward', the fleet set sail in some haste.

From internal evidence, this surviving journal of the
raid was written on board the *Primrose* but the author's
identity is not known. The course of the expedition is
traced from the Cape Verde Islands to the West Indies
and the seizure of Cartagena on 11 January 1586. There
in a diversionary attack, the author recalls how 'wee
had the rowther [*i.e.* rudder] of our pinnasse stroke

awaie, & mens hattes from thire heades, & the topp of
our meane maste beaten in peeces, the oares striken owte
of our menes hands as they rowed, & our Captaine like to
have bin slaine (f. 171ᵛ).

Forced to leave Cartagena Drake then sailed for St
Augustine (San Augustin) in Florida which he sacked
and thence to Virginia to assist the colonists settled by
Sir Walter Raleigh at Roanoke in 1585.

113 An itinerary of the voyage

> 'A discourse of Syr Francis Drake's voiage,
> wh[ich] by god's grace he shall well pfomeme [*i.e.*
> perform]. The 25th April 1586.'
> 28 × 21 cm   *Lansdowne MS 100, f. 98a–b*

This account of the voyage seems to be a provisional
report on Drake's raid up to the time of the sacking of
Santiago on 4 November 1585. There it records that as
the inhabitants had 'denyed him water, he spoiled the
cyttye, rased th[e] [defences?], and brought awaye lx
peeces of Brasse . . .'.

After this date the author of the report confines his

account to what he thought Drake's future plans for the West Indies would be. In view of his apparently intimate knowledge of these plans, he was presumably in Drake's confidence, and had sailed perhaps on the voyage as far as Santiago or else had met the English fleet there. After taking Cartagena, Drake was to meet a force of 5,000 'Semyroanes' (*i.e.* Cimaroons) at Nombre de Dios who were to accompany him up the river Chagres to take Panama. 'The towne of Panamaw standeth upon the sea coast in the Southe Sea, and dothe [contain?] all the treasure that cometh by water from the newe kingdom of Perow [*i.e.* Peru], which maye be taken without resistance, this towne maye bee a praye of a myllyon of ducatts.' In the event Drake did not proceed with the plan to take Panama.

114 The burning of Santiago

A plan-view of the attack by Sir Francis Drake on the island of Santiago in the Cape Verde Islands on 17 November 1585.
MS coloured on vellum.
69 × 78 cm   *Egerton MS 2579*

On 16 November 1585 the fleet anchored off the island of Santiago in the Cape Verde Islands between the towns of Praya and Santiago. A thousand men or more under the command of Carleill were put ashore. Thomas Cates's edition of Bigges's journal (included by Hakluyt in his *Principal Navigations*), recorded that: 'The place where we had first to march did affourd no good order, for the ground was mountainous and full of dales . . . butt such was his industrious disposition [*i.e.* Carleill's], as he would never leave, until wee had gotte up to a faire plain, where we made stand for the assembling of the army.' The army was then divided into three companies, two of which marched to the tune of fife and drum as depicted in the view. The town of Santiago, lying in a rocky and steeply inclined valley, was soon taken and the Spanish garrison fled. After a stay of fourteen days the fleet departed for 'there was not found any treasure at all, or any thing else of worth besides'. In revenge for great wrongs suffered by 'old M. William Hawkins' four years previously the town was burnt to the ground.

Although unsigned this map is usually attributed to the work of Baptista Boazio who drew the plans, which were later engraved to accompany the various editions of Bigges's journal. Amongst the engravings is one showing the attack on Santiago (illustrated) which may be based on this manuscript. Unlike this manuscript plan, however, which depicts faithfully Carleill's division of the army into three parts, the engraver has shown the soldiers in a different formation; he has also placed the English fleet before the town of Santiago rather than to the eastern end of the island. These discrepancies make it difficult to ascribe the manuscript plan to Boazio with any certainty, although the two plans are obviously very similar.

EXPEDITIO
FRANCISCI DRAKI
EQVITIS ANGLI
IN
INDIAS OCCIDENTALES
A. M. D. LXXXV.

Quâ vrbes, Fanum D. Iacobi, D. Dominici, D. Auguftini & Carthagena, captæ fuére.

Additis paßim regionum locorúmque omnium tabulis Geographicis quàm accuratißimis.

LEYDÆ,
Apud Fr. Raphelengium.
M. D. LXXXVIII.

115

115 The earliest edition of the West Indies Voyage

Expeditio Francisci Draki Equitis Angli in Indias Occidentales A.M.D. LXXXV. Quâ urbes, Fanum D. Iacobi, D. Dominici, D. Augustini & Carthagena, captae fuêre . . . Leydae, Apud Fr. Raphelengium, 1588.
22 cm   *G. 6511*

The author of this account, Walter Bigges, was Captain-Lieutenant of Carleill's company of soldiers. On his death at Cartagena the journal was finished by Lieutenant Crofts. The first editions of the journal were in Latin and French and were published in 1588. Although both editions call for accompanying maps on their title-pages, only the Latin edition seems to have actually included the four large battle plans drawn by Baptista Boazio. These are described below (**117–19**).

Of the surviving examples of the Latin edition the present copy alone is recorded as having the maps. A note attached to the fly-leaf in the hand of Thomas Grenville (1755–1846), who bequeathed this book with his library to the Trustees of the British Museum, describes this copy as follows: 'This is the earliest & best edition that I have seen of Drake's W. Ind: Voyage, with 4 maps, very rare.' The maps (the stubs of which can clearly be seen) were folded and placed at the end of the text. These were subsequently removed and laid flat in a bound portfolio (*G. 345★*).

An Italian artist living in London, Baptista Boazio (fl. 1588–1606) made five maps to illustrate Drake's voyage to the West Indies. Four depict the major cities which were raided – Santiago, San Domingo, Cartagena and San Augustin. None of these maps, which are the first known printed views of the towns, is signed by Boazio. The fifth map is a general chart of the 'Famous West Indian voyage' and bears the inscription 'By Baptista B.' Apart from this the only contemporary source for Boazio's authorship of the maps comes from the title-page of the second English edition of Walter Bigges's *A Summarie and true discourse . . .*, printed in London by Roger Ward in 1589. Here it is stated that the volume includes 'Geographicall Mappes exactly describing each of the Tovvnes with their scituations, and the maner of the Armies approaching to the vvinning of them: diligently made by Baptista Boazio'. Boazio is well known for having made several manuscript maps, notably of Cadiz 1596, Azores 1597, and Ireland 1599. He is not known to have been an engraver and there is no evidence to support the theory that he engraved the maps of the West Indies; it has been suggested tentatively that the engraver was Jodocus Hondius. There is no indication that Boazio acquired his information by accompanying Drake on the voyage.

The four city maps were issued in two sizes. The larger, *ca* 40 × 52 cm, include Latin inscriptions and were almost certainly published in the Latin edition of Bigges's *Summarie*, Leyden, 1588. Those which were issued with the Grenville copy of this edition (*G.6511*) have a Latin text pasted on to the bottom border, and other copies from an English edition of 1589 are known, with English texts. The reduced maps, *ca* 20 × 30 cm, with captions in Latin and French, were issued with some editions of *A Summarie*. It is not certain whether the general map was intended to be published with Bigges's work, although two copies are known to have the map bound in. The British Library examples are to be found in the German edition of 1589 (**118b**).

116 The West Indies raid on a map

> The famous West Indian voyadge made by the Englishe fleete . . . wherein were gotten the Townes of S.t Iago: S.to Domingo, Cartagena and S.t Augustines . . . the whole course of the saide Viadge beinge plainlie described by the pricked line. Newlie come forth by Baptista B.
> 49 × 54 cm   *G.6509*

This map, drawn by Baptista Boazio in England from reports of the voyage, shows the route of Drake's ships in his raid on Spanish America in 1585–6. The fleet is also shown calling at the English colony of Roanoke in June 1586, claimed for England on the map by the flag of St George. Boazio has included a picture of a 'Sea

Cornye' or Trigger fish in the bottom left-hand corner, copied from the drawings of the artist, John White.

The map appears to have been issued as a broadside, although one copy of it occurs in Bigges's *Summarie and true discourse of Sir Frances Drakes West Indian Voyage* (London, R. Field, 1589), and the style resembles that of the battle plans which accompany Bigges's book.

117 The attack on San Domingo, 1586

> Civitas S Dominici sita in Hispaniola Indica Angliae magnitudine fere aequalis, ipsa vrbs elegantor ab Hispanis extructa. et omnibus circumvicinis insulis iura dat. [Leyden, 1588.]
> 40 × 55 cm   *G.345★*

Once the capital of Spanish America, San Domingo had long since declined in wealth and importance. Yet in the 1580s it was still one of the largest settlements in the West Indies and was Drake's first target for attack. He met with little resistance. Spain's warning of Drake's imminent arrival had failed to reach San Domingo, whose approaches were ill-defended. On the seaward side a poorly equipped fort guarded the port, while on the landward side the city was virtually defenceless because it was believed impossible to land a force on that coast.

Guided by the pilot of a captured Spanish bark, Drake's fleet landed at the mouth of the River Hayna. Ten miles west of the city, it was the one place where a landing was possible. Here Carleill disembarked with 800 men who attacked San Domingo before the Spaniards were aware of them. Ruthlessly sacking the city, Drake discovered that he had overestimated its wealth and the yields of silver, gold and silks proved disappointing. His initial demand of a million ducats' ransom was finally reduced to 25,000, which the Spanish agreed to pay.

Depicting the raid on San Domingo, this map was published in the first edition of *Expeditio Francisci Draki . . .*, 1588. A Latin legend, pasted to the bottom border, relates to the key letters printed on the map.

118 Drake captures Cartagena, 1586

> **a** Civitas Carthagena in Indiæ occidentalis continente sita, portu commodissimo, ad mercaturam inter Hispaniam et Peru exercendam. [Leyden, 1588.]
> 41 × 55 cm   *G.345★*

Leaving San Domingo on 1 February 1586, Drake arrived at Cartagena on the 9th. The most important city in the Caribbean, Cartagena was the storage centre for gold, pearls, hides, cochineal and other produce of the Main brought there by local shipping. Difficult of access, the city was also weakly defended and a 'vigorous

117

118a

119

assult served to turn the position'. Drake's forces immediately pillaged the town and set fire to several buildings before a 107,000 ducat ransom saved the remaining houses from a similar fate.

Drake remained in Cartagena for over two months. His men were ravaged by sickness and news of an advancing armada lowered morale even further. After consultations with his captains, Drake decided to abandon his intention to go to Panama. He left Cartagena on 24 April taking with him some 200 Turks, Moors and negro slaves. Contrary to Spanish expectations, he did not raid Havana but set off for Virginia.

Oriented with east at the top this map clearly shows the narrow isthmus, 150 paces wide, across which the English forces pushed into Cartagena. Published in the first edition of *Expeditio Francisci Draki* 1588 this map bears a Latin legend pasted to the bottom border.

b   Civitas Cartagena in Indiæ Occidentalis continente sita, portu commodissimo ad mercaturam inter Hispaniam et Peru exercendam. In: *Relation oder Beschreibung des Rheiss und Schiffart aus Engellandt . . .* (1589).
20 × 30 cm   G.6576

The present plan is one of a set of four smaller versions

of the large engraved battle plans which were published in the Latin edition of Drake's 'West Indian Voyage' at Leyden in 1588. The engraving includes in the lower margin a descriptive caption in Latin but, although the plan bears reference numbers at particular places, an accompanying explanatory table is not present.

It has been suggested that this set of smaller engraved plans, after the drawings of Boazio, may have been intended for inclusion in the Latin and French editions of Drake's 'West Indian Voyage' 1588, but no example of such a copy is recorded. Only one copy of the 1588 Latin edition is known to include maps at all and these are of the larger version (see **118**).

119   San Augustin burnt

S Augustini pars est terræ Florida sub latitudine 30 gradora vero maritimta humilior est, lancinata et insulosa.
46 × 55 cm   G.345*

San Augustin, the oldest Spanish settlement in North America, had been established in 1565 by Pedro Menéndez de Avilés. On 28 May 1586 Drake sighted the look-out beacon at San Augustin (point *C* on the plan). Taking a number of pinnaces and a company of men, Drake made for the wooden fort of St John (point *I* on the plan). They were surprised to find a Protestant Frenchman, whom the Spanish had previously captured, sitting 'in a little boate, playing on his phiph [i.e. fife] to the tune of the Prince of Orenge his song'. He informed them that the Spanish had deserted the fort, which Drake then promptly seized together with some two thousand pounds of bullion. The company marched to the town of San Augustin which they burnt to the ground before sailing to Virginia to help the English colonists.

This engraved map, like the other three battle plans, was first published in *Expeditio Francisci Draki* 1588.

120 The Roanoke colony relieved

A summarie and true discourse of Sir Fraunces Drakes West Indian Voyage. [Begun by Walter Bigges, continued by Lieutenant Crofts.] London, R. Field, 1589.
20 cm   G.6509

In this popular narrative of Drake's raid on the West Indies and Spanish Main in 1585–6, Drake's arrival at Roanoke Island and his offer to Raleigh's 'Virginia' colonists to leave a ship or to take them back to England are described. 'Maister Lane [i.e. Ralph Lane the colony's governor] with those of the chiefest of his companie he had then with him, considering what should be best for them to doe, made request unto the generall under their handes, that they might have passage for England.' Drake took off the 103 settlers on 18 June 1586 and set sail for Portsmouth.

The engraved maps in the book are decorated with sketches of zoological subjects, evidently derived from the drawings of John White who was repatriated in the fleet with the other colonists.

121 An iguana

Igwano. Water colour on paper.
20 × 20 cm
Lent by B.M. Department of Prints and Drawings,
L.B.1 (73)

This drawing by White may be compared with the inset of the engraved plan of Cartagena from Walter Bigges's *Summarie and true discourse of Sir Frances Drakes West Indian Voyage* (1589).

The unknown author of the maps which illustrate Bigges's account evidently had access to White's material, for several animals and fishes after the artist's drawings appear in the maps, including the iguana.

122

122 John White's map of Virginia

'La Virgenia Pars'. A map drawn by John White *ca* 1585. 10 miles [= 4 cm].
MS coloured on paper. 40 × 20 cm
Lent by the B.M. Department of Prints & Drawings,
L.B.1(2)

This detailed map of the region between Chesapeake Bay and Cape Lookout is based on the surveys of the mathematician Thomas Harriot (1560–1621), a member of the short-lived Roanoke settlement of 1585–6, and of his fellow colonist John White (fl. 1584–93). White was an artist and later governor of the 1587 colony, whose duties included surveying and draughting this map. The island of Roanoke (spelt 'Roanoac') is clearly shown within the Outer Banks. The Royal Arms and those of Raleigh who promoted the colony are also depicted.

Theodore de Bry used a modified drawing by White of the map of the same area for his stylized engraving in the first volume of his *America* (1590), which contains Harriot's *A brief and true report* of the colony in Virginia.

XI

Drake and the Spanish Armada

IN 1586 Santa Cruz, the Captain General of the Spanish fleet, dubbed the force that was to sail against England the 'Felicissima Armada'. Overwork and worry about the preparations for this great Armada hastened his death and, before the Armada sailed, command of it had to be given to a new Captain General. He was Don Alonso Perez de Guzman, 7th Duke of Medina Sidonia. His second-in-command was Juan Martinez de Recalde. Despite the attempt to forestall the Armada by Drake in the Spring of 1587, the Spanish fleet set sail from Lisbon for England in mid-May 1588. The Spanish plan was that the Armada would rendezvous with Alexander Farnese, Duke of Parma, who had a large army, possibly as many as 30,000 men, waiting in the Netherlands. The fleet would cover Parma's Channel crossing to England, and then combine the troops carried by the Armada with Parma's army to invade England.

In England the local militias were being trained and armed to resist a landing. The fleet was victualled and put on a war footing under Lord Howard of Effingham, Lord High Admiral of England since 1585, and Lord Henry Seymour, Admiral of the Fleet in the Narrow Seas. Drake was appointed second-in-command to Howard. John Hawkins, Sir William Wynter and Martin Frobisher were given subordinate commands. The English Command were still debating in Plymouth whether they should sail for Spain and fight the Armada in its own waters or await its arrival off the English coast, when the news that the Armada had been sighted near the Scilly Isles was brought to Drake. He was playing bowls on Plymouth Hoe, according to the legend, on 19 July 1588, and he gave the characteristic reply 'We have time enough to finish the game and beat the Spaniards, too.' There is no contemporary authority for the tale of the game of bowls; the earliest record is dated nearly half a century later. Presumably Howard, as Lord High Admiral, would have been the recipient of the message rather than Drake, but Francis Drake captured popular English imagination as the vanquisher of the Spaniards. Likewise, in Spanish history and literature the Armada's defeat is seen as the work of 'El Draque'.

As soon as the Armada was seen, beacons were lit on the headlands along the coast to give warning of the enemy. Howard sailed his fleet out of Plymouth and the two fleets exchanged fire on 21 July. Spanish progress up Channel became a nine days' running battle, with the English fleet sailing round the crescent formation of the Armada but unable to make any significant impression on it. There were two notable engagements off Portland Bill and the Isle of Wight, but when the Armada anchored off Calais on 27 July it had lost only two ships.

Philip II, King of Spain, by an unknown artist, *ca.* 1580. (*National Portrait Gallery no. 347*).

The English had used Drake's western fleet to prevent the Armada landing in England and had deployed Seymour's eastern fleet to immobilize Parma. Once off Calais the western fleet was joined by the eastern, and on the evening of the 28th the English sent in fireships amongst the Armada. Medina Sidonia ordered cables to be cut to allow his ships to move out of the path of the fireships. By the morning of the 29th, the Armada, except for Medina Sidonia's flagship, the *San Martin*, and a few other vessels, was scattered from Calais to Gravelines. Drake and Seymour attacked and the battle of Gravelines was fought. On the morning of 30 July Medina Sidonia was still trying to re-form his battered Armada, but it was in danger of being driven on to the sandbanks off Zeeland. Then, providentially for the Spanish, the wind changed to west-south-west, enabling them to sail north and take flight.

Drake and Howard followed them as far as the Firth of Forth and then turned back for home. Not a single English ship had been lost. Back in England an invasion by Parma was still expected and on 8 and 9 August Queen Elizabeth I reviewed her troops drawn up at Tilbury ready to resist a possible invasion force.

On 10 August the Armada rounded the Orkneys and ran into Atlantic gales which wrecked half of them, scattering their timbers and their unfortunate crews round the northern shores of Scotland and off the coast of Ireland. The other half limped back to Spain which they reached by the beginning of 1589. The good news reached England, and on 20 August a service of thanksgiving was held in London to rejoice at Protestant England's deliverance from the might of Catholic Spain.

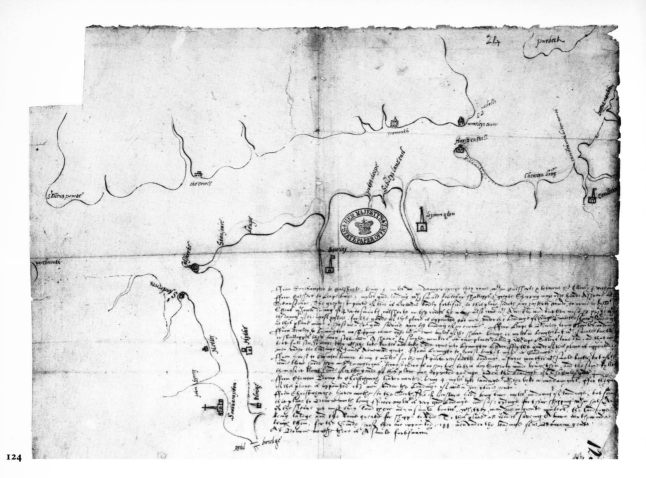

123 The attack on Cadiz

Plan of the attack on Cadiz on 19 April 1587
MS Coloured on paper.
36 × 46 cm   *Lent by the P.R.O. MPF 318*
(formerly SP 12/202 no. 14)

Drawn by Drake's vice-admiral, William Borough, who
was also Clerk of the Queen's Ships and a noted chart-
maker, the plan shows the course of the English fleet's
attack on sixty or so merchantmen at Cadiz. Drake set
sail for the Iberian coast on 2 April 1587 with
instructions, as Borough reminded him in the letter
which accompanied this map: 'that you with these ships
now under your charge, should come hither to this Cape
[*i.e.* St Vincent], and upon this coast, and seek by all the
best means you can to impeach their [*i.e.* the Spaniards']
purpose and stop their meeting at Lisbon...'. Critical of
Drake's interpretation of these instructions and his
high-handed methods, Borough soon found himself
accused of mutiny but, unlike Doughty, influential
friends saved him from Drake's wrath.

At Cadiz, Drake led an attack on the merchantmen
and destroyed 'a ship of the Margues of Sᵗᵃ Crus' which
he found in the inner harbour (point 'h' in the plan). In

all about twenty-two ships were 'sunk and taken without
any resistance, whereof he carried away with him six
which he spoiled upon the seas, and after sunk them
also', as an Englishman then in Spain recorded. To
complete his raid on Spanish shipping, Drake succeeded
in capturing a carrack off the Azores, laden with East
Indies produce valued officially at £114,000.

124 England's defences against invasion

Map of the coast from Portsmouth to Purbeck,
including Southampton Water and the north coast
of the Isle of Wight from St Helens to the
Needles. [1587.]
MS Pen and ink on paper.
42 × 32 cm   *Lent by the P.R.O. MPF 135*
(Removed from State Papers Domestic Elizabeth I
SP 12/199 no. 23.)

England put herself in readiness in 1587 to withstand the
threat of a Spanish invasion. The map contains a
description of the landing places on the south coast with
the numbers of men to defend them and the names of
those placed in command.

125 Impressions made from Sir George Carey's seal matrix.

125 The Isle of Wight

Ivory seal matrix of Sir George Carey
(1547–1603) as Captain of the Isle of Wight and
Vice-Admiral of Southampton; dated about 1586.
  The matrix has two faces connected by a
moulded conical handle. On one face is a man-of-
war with the mainsail bearing the Carey arms, and
on the other is the shield of arms of the Carey
family.
Diam. (larger face) 8.8 cm; (smaller face) 8.45 cm
*Lent by B.M. Department of Medieval and Later
Antiquities, 1944, 6–1, 1*

Sir George Carey was Captain of the Isle of Wight from
1582 to 1603. In February 1587 Elizabeth I had
intelligence of a design for a surprise attack on the Isle of
Wight and she authorized Carey to take view and muster
of the trained bands in certain hundreds of Hampshire
for the defence of the island. When the Armada
threatened the island in late July 1588 he was vigilant in
its defence, sending four ships and two pinnaces to assist
the Lord Admiral's fleet. He watched the engagement of
the two fleets on 25 July off the Island and declared that
it was carried on '. . . with so great expense of powder and
bullet that the shot continued so thick together that it
might have been judged a skirmish with small shot on
land than a fight with great shot on sea.'

126 Drake's plans to defeat the Spanish

Sir Francis Drake to Queen Elizabeth, Plymouth
13 April 1588.
MS 33 × 23 cm
Lent by the P.R.O., S.P. 12/209 no. 89

The letter outlines measures to repel the Armada now
assembled in Lisbon. Much depends on 'the resolucyon
of our owne people'. He has never in all his life known
better men or of more gallant minds. There was never
any force so strong as this Spanish fleet but 'the Lord of
all strengthes is stronger and will defend the trowth of
his word for his own names sake'. He advised that the
fleet under his charge should be augmented, provisioned
and then attack the enemy on his own coasts.

127 The English fleet

The Ark Royal.
Woodcut. 51 × 74 cm
*Lent by B.M. Department of Prints and Drawings,
1874-8-8-1367*

The *Ark Royal* was built for Sir Walter Raleigh in 1581
and was originally known as the *Ark Raleigh*. She was
renamed the *Ark Royal* when acquired by the Crown
and was then used as the flagship for Charles, Lord
Howard of Effingham, Lord High Admiral of England.
  Drake captained the *Revenge*, launched in 1575. She
was 92 feet long, 32 feet in beam, displaced 450 tons,
carried almost 50 guns and required some 250 crew –
mariners and gunners. John Hawkins had been largely
responsible for the building of the new-style navy in the
1570s and 1580s, and although the Spanish and English
fleets were roughly matched in size and gunpower, the
manoeuvrability of the new English vessels and their
better-trained crews sailing in home waters proved to be
decisive factors.

128 The English fleet

A Note of all the Shippes now at the Seas Vnder
the chardge of the Lo. Admirall [Howard], wth
their nombers of men, and tyme of Victualinge,
4 July 1588.
MS 35 × 24 cm
Lent by the P.R.O., SP 12/213 no. 2(i)

This note was enclosed in a letter from Marmaduke
Darell to Lord Burghley, written at Plymouth on 22 July
1588. The first sheet of this list of ships is exhibited.
Sloane MS 2450 (not shown) is a record of the
'expences' of the English fleet in 1588. A similar list of
victuals and supplies belonging to the ships serving in
the Spanish fleet, 1587, was drawn up in the *Libro de
Cargos (Pepys MS 2269)*.

127

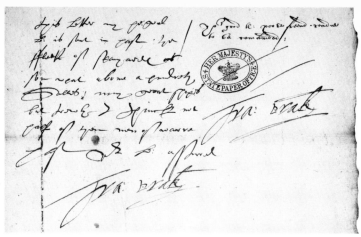

129

129 The 21st of July

Sir Francis Drake to Lord Henry Seymour,
Admiral of the Fleet in the Narrow Seas or Sir
William Wynter, off the Start, 21 July 1588.
MS 31 × 24 cm

Lent by the P.R.O., S.P. 12/212 no. 82

When the news reached Howard and Drake on 19 July in
Plymouth that the Armada had been sighted off the
Lizard there was some danger of the western fleet being
boxed in. They managed to sail, however, and on 21 July
Drake wrote from on board the *Revenge* at the direction
of the Lord Admiral [Howard] to report contact with the
Armada. Drake asked Seymour and Wynter to put the
ships serving under their charge in readiness to assist
against the Armada. The postscript (in Drake's hand)
adds '. . . the Fleet of Spanyards at sea . . . aboue a
hundreth Sales many great ships, but trowth I thinck
not half of them men of warre'.

130 The Fight

Wax impression of the seal of Charles, Lord
Howard of Effingham, Lord High Admiral of
England, 1585.
Diam 12.2 cm

Lent by the National Maritime Museum

The seal design shows a two-decked man-of-war of the
reign of Queen Elizabeth I; on the mainsail, the shield of
the arms of Howard encircled by the Garter.

Howard was Lord High Admiral from 1585 to 1619.
Drake became his vice-admiral in 1588. They
commanded the western fleet which from 21 to 27 July
1588 failed to wreak more than superficial damage on the
Armada despite two notable engagements, off Portland
Bill on 23 July and off the Isle of Wight on 25 July.
Howard, however, did prevent the Spanish from
establishing a base of operations in the Isle of Wight.

131 Gravelines, 27–29 July

A contemporary engraving of the battle of
Gravelines in: Jean Orlers *La Genealogie des
illustres Comtes de Nassau*, Deuxième Edition.
Amsterdam, 1624, plate between pp. 60–61.
23 × 30 cm   G.929

The Spanish fleet is shown fleeing in confusion, closely
followed by the English, past Gravelines on the Flemish
coast; Calais and Dover are shown in the background.
The accompanying text gives a lengthy account of the
events of 29 July 1588 when the fleets were fighting off
the coast of the Netherlands. Contemporary representations of the battle are rare. This engraving is also to
be found in the first edition of this work, published in
1612.

Drake and Howard anchored a mile off Calais on 27
July and were joined by Seymour and his eastern fleet.
On the evening of the 28th they launched fireships
carrying lighted faggots, pitch and tar into the Armada,
one of which exploded. At this Medina Sidonia took
fright, for three years earlier at the siege of Antwerp
infernal delayed-action machines – boats packed with
gunpowder and lit by slow-burning fuses – had killed
more than a thousand Spanish. He ordered his men to
cut the ships' cables in order to escape from the path of
the fireships. By the morning of the 29th the Armada
had been scattered to the north-east of Calais, their best
anchors left on the sea-bed. Drake and Seymour
attacked and chased the Spaniards out of the Channel.
The Spanish had now no chance of linking up with
Parma, indeed by the morning of 30 July a north-west
wind threatened to force them on to the Zeeland
sandbanks. The English gave up the chase, fearful of
being driven on the banks as well. By the 31st the wind
had changed to west-south-west and allowed the
battered Armada to flee due north.

132 In the North Sea

Decision by the English Council of War to pursue
the Armada, 1 August 1588

28 × 20 cm   *Additional MS 33740, f. 6*

The Armada had taken flight northwards. On 31 July
Seymour and Wynter took the eastern fleet to cruise off
the Thames to block Parma if he dared to come out into
the Channel. The Council of War were fearful lest the
Armada put in on the east coast of England or Scotland
for water, or supplies, or to re-form for a further attack,
so they 'agreede . . . to folowe and pursue the Spanishe
Fleete untill we haue cleared oure owne coaste.' The
resolution was signed by the Lord High Admiral of
England, Charles, Lord Howard of Effingham; George
Clifford, Earl of Cumberland, who commanded the
Elizabeth Bonaventure; Lord Thomas Howard, later
first Earl of Suffolk, who had been knighted at sea for his
valour on 26 July 1588 (together with Lord Sheffield,
John Hawkins, Martin Frobisher and two others) and
afterwards made captain of a man-of-war; Edmund,
Lord Sheffield, who commanded the *White Bear*; Sir
Francis Drake; Sir Edward Hoby (1560–1617), nephew
of William Cecil; Sir John Hawkins and captain
Thomas Fenner.

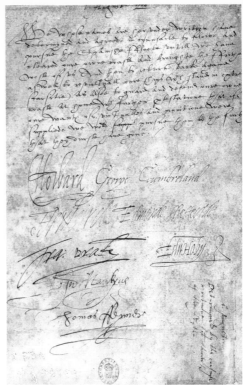

132

131

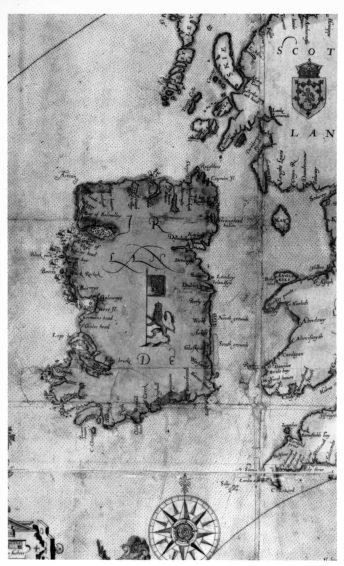

133 The ships of the Spanish Armada wrecked off the coasts of Scotland and Ireland (detail from *Maps C.7 c.1(2) no. 11*).

133 The end of the Armada in Ireland

A Discourse concerning the Spanishe fleete invadinge England in the yeere 1588 . . . written in Italian by Petruccio Ubaldini . . . and translated by A. Ryther [London, 1590] p. 25.
18 cm   292.e.9.(1)

Once they had passed the Firth of Forth the badly damaged ships of the Armada were shadowed as far as the Orkneys by only a couple of English ships. Howard and Drake turned the western fleet back to England, secure in the knowledge that Medina Sidonia was taking the northern route back to Spain.

On 10 August the Armada rounded the Orkneys safely, but then ran into Atlantic gales which sank

vessels or drove them on to the rocks and headlands of the northern coast of Scotland and the west coast of Ireland. Such captains as sought a haven on the west coast of Ireland, looking for food and water for their sickly and often severely wounded crews and a safe anchorage in which to carry out repairs to their badly damaged ships, were given an almost unanimously hostile reception by the local population. Petruccio Ubaldini, in this extract, recorded that 'The persons lost in Ireland were esteemed to be about 5500.' Casualties certainly ran into thousands. By the end of the year half the ships of the Armada had returned to Spain; the other half had gone to the bottom of the ocean. A set of twelve accompanying charts illustrating the course of the Armada was engraved by the English translator of Ubaldini's work, Augustine Ryther.

134 Tilbury

a   The Queen visits the army

The Queenes visiting of the Campe at Tilburie
with her entertainment there. T.D. [*i.e.* Thomas
Deloney] London, 1588.

41 × 31 cm   *C.18.e.2.(64)*

An army had been raised in response to the threat from
the Spanish. On 24 July Elizabeth conferred the title of
Lieutenant and Captain-General of the Queen's Armies
and Companies upon her favourite, Robert Dudley, Earl
of Leicester, (1532?–1588). After the battle of
Gravelines the Queen feared Parma might still attempt
an invasion, so to hearten her troops, and see Leicester,
she set off on 8 August along the Thames to Tilbury fort,
to the north of which the troops were encamped ready to
resist the enemy should they land.

At Tilbury she was said to have '. . . passed like some
Amazonian empress through all her army' and to have
addressed them in the following terms

> . . . I am come amongst you . . . being resolved in the
> midst and heat of battle, to live or die amongst you
> all, to lay down for my God and for my kingdom,
> and for my people, my honour and my blood, even
> in the dust. I know I have . . . the heart and stomach
> of a king, and of a king of England too, and think
> foul scorn that Parma or Spain, or any prince of
> Europe should dare to invade the borders of my
> realm.

Elizabeth's gesture was widely reported. This
broadside, celebrating the events of 8 and 9 August, was
entered in the Stationers' Company Register on 10
August. It was the work of Thomas Deloney, the ballad-
writer and pamphleteer.

b   Pictorial chart of the Thames estuary from
Lambeth to Tilbury Hope, by Robert Adams,
Surveyor of the Works, showing the route for
Queen Elizabeth I's journey to, and from,
Tilbury, 8–10 August 1588, when she inspected
the army assembled there against the Spanish
Armada; 1588.
Pen-drawn; scale 1 inch to 1 mile with South at
the top and coloured in wash.

11 × 70 cm   *Additional MS 44839*

The chart resembles closely, and is presumably based
upon, another one made by Robert Adams in the same
year, on which the defences erected along the course of
the Thames to protect London in the event of an
invasion attempt by the Spanish are delineated. The
latter is now preserved in the King George III's
Topographical Collection (K. Top. VI.17). The present
chart as well as showing the gun batteries and other
fortifications contains additional information. For
example, a 'Pricked Line' marks the route taken by the
Queen to, and from, Tilbury. A list in the left margin
lettered A to E refers to features of interest.

135 The Armada Badge

An electrotype of 'Dangers Averted', 1589.
5 × 4.75 cm
Lent by B.M. Department of Coins and Medals

The gold badge from which this electrotype has been
made was executed shortly after the defeat of the
Armada, probably by Nicholas Hilliard and possibly as a
naval reward. Cast and chased: with rings for
suspension.

On the obverse is a bust of Elizabeth almost full face,
crowned. The legend: *Ditior in toto non alter circulus
orbe* (no other circle in the whole world more rich), refers
to the power of the Queen's crown which, after the
defeat of the Armada, was thought equal to any crown in
Europe. The reverse shows a bay-tree uninjured by
lightning and winds, flourishing upon an island,
inscribed *non ipsa pericula tangunt* (not even dangers
affect it), and two ships in the distance. The device of
the reverse refers to the imputed virtues of the laurel or
bay-tree, which was deemed incapable of injury from
lightning and also protected the places where it grew, or
the persons who wore it.

136 A commemorative Medal, 1588

An Armada medal.
Diam. 5 cm   *Lent by BM Department of
Coins and Medals 1950-8-5-3; M.6897*

The Armada was the first historical event for which
medals were struck by an English sovereign. The
obverse of this medal shows Pope, kings, bishops and
others seated in consultation with bandaged eyes; the
floor filled with spikes and has the legend *Durum est
contra stimulos calcitrare* (It is hard to kick against the
pricks – *Acts* IX.5). It is a satirical representation of the
vain efforts of the Pope, Philip II and other princes who
had confederated against Elizabeth I. The reverse shows
the Spanish fleet driven against rocks and has the legend
Tu Deus Magnus et Magna facis tu solus Deus (Thou,
God, art great and doest wondrous things; thou art God
alone – *Psalm* 86). Thus the destruction of the Spanish
Armada was ascribed to Divine intervention.

136

XII

The last voyage of Drake and Hawkins

HALF the ships of the Armada, though badly damaged, had reached the ports of northern Spain by early 1589; England feared another invasion attempt. A joint stock expedition with Drake commanding the ships and Sir John Norris (1547–1597) commanding the soldiers was mounted in 1589. The plan was to repeat Drake's successful Cadiz raid of 1587 on a grander scale. The surviving Armada ships in Corunna, San Sebastian and Santander were to be destroyed, a revolt in Lisbon against Philip II was to be raised and the Azores occupied.

The fleet sailed in April 1589 and was dogged by ill luck. A few Armada ships were sunk at Corunna. The Earl of Essex, who had joined Norris, failed to take Lisbon. Drake captured sixty supply ships at Cascaes and sacked Vigo, but returned to England in July without making an attempt on the Azores. Several thousand members of the expedition died, chiefly of disease, and the backers of the venture were out of pocket.

Drake spent the next few years ashore busying himself in the west country and at Westminster. He was responsible for providing Plymouth with a fresh water supply and sat in the Parliament of 1593 for Plymouth. As early as 1593 an expedition to the West Indies by Drake and Hawkins was mooted but it was late August 1595 before they set sail. They had with them rather less than a thousand soldiers under the command of Sir Thomas Baskerville and about 1,500 sailors. The aims of the expedition were twofold: to capture 'tow myllyons and a hallf of tresure' which was aboard a crippled Spanish galleon lying helpless 'unrygged and her ordenance put a shore' in the harbour of San Juan, Puerto Rico; and to sack Panama. Initially they may have contemplated capturing and holding the Isthmus of Panama, thus disrupting Spain's main treasure-route, but this idea had been abandoned before they left England.

They did not reach San Juan, Puerto Rico, until November 1595, by which time it had been fortified against them and the treasure removed from the Spanish galleon. On 12 November 1595, off Puerto Rico, Hawkins died. Drake was obliged to abandon his attempt on San Juan and made for his second objective. He was no luckier there. Nombre de Dios fell to him early on 27 December but those whom he took prisoner told him '. . . that havinge intelligence longe before of our [*i.e.* Drake's and Baskerville's] cominge theyr treasure was conveyed to places of more safetie, eyther to panama or secretly hidden. . .'. On 29 December therefore Baskerville marched the soldiers towards Panama, straight into an ambush. They were 'enforced to retire' and took to the sea again on 5 January. Once they were afloat the weather became 'stormie and blusterous' so that little progress was made. Many men died, Nombre de Dios having the reputation of being 'the sickliest place of the Indies' and on 28 January 1596 'wtin 8 or 9 leagues of Numbre de dios', at Porto Bello, Drake died.

Baskerville took over command of the enterprise and decided to sail for home. The news of Drake's death was brought to England by the fleet in April 1596.

138

137 The Drake–Norris episode

Ephemeris expeditionis Norreysij & Draki in Lusitaniam. Londini, Impensis Thomae Woodcocke, 1589.
19 cm   *C.32 f. 24*

This diary of the Drake–Norris expedition covers the period 15 March to 3 July 1589. It was probably an English propaganda publication and is one of the most important sources for the history of the English attack on Spain and Portugal in 1589. The defeat of the Spanish Armada in 1588 did not herald the end of war with Spain. In April 1589 the Drake–Norris expedition set sail for northern Spain with Sir John Norris (1547–97) in command of the soldiery and Sir Francis Drake commanding the fleet. Their objectives were to locate and destroy the ships of the Armada that had managed to return to Spain; raise a revolt in Lisbon against Philip II who was now King of Portugal as well as King of Spain; and seize the Azores. They failed to secure these objectives: only a few Spanish ships were destroyed, Lisbon did not yield to the English troops and a contrary wind precluded an attempt on the Azores. The expedition returned to England in July 1589 having lost several thousand men, mainly through disease. It had also lost, rather than made, money for its financial backers who included the Queen.

138 Drake in Devon

Plymouth harbour and the country inland to Tavistock, *ca* 1590.
40 × 31 cm   *Cotton MS Augustus I.i, 41*

This map showing the conduit or leat built to supply Plymouth with fresh water is half the size of an almost identical map in the library of the Marquess of Salisbury at Hatfield House. The Hatfield map was possibly drawn from a survey by Robert Lampen, who received payment in 1589–90 from Plymouth Corporation 'for Planynge and vewinge the ground for the water course from mevie [*i.e.* River Meavy] for vj dayes'.

Both maps have mile-figures marked along the conduit from the River Meavy to Plymouth. A legend on the Hatfield map, but lacking on the Cotton map, states that 'From the Fyrst taking in of the river, that is now brought into plimouth (as it is carried everie waie to get the vantage of the hilles) is by measure 27 miles after 1000 paces to a mile and fyve foot a pace.' That is to say, the measurements of the Surveyor are according to the Roman mile.

The project to bring fresh water to Plymouth was discussed in the Parliament of 1584 but work does not seem to have started until 1589–90. Drake had been a member of the special Parliamentary Committee to which the project had been referred and it was he who undertook, for a price, to bring the water of the Meavy to

Plymouth by tapping it at the 'head weare', before it ran any risk of contamination in the lower reaches.

This map is drawn in pictorial style with coasts and topographical details represented in perspective. Plymouth Sound is carefully depicted. Churches and country houses are delineated with precision – Buckland Abbey is marked 'Sr. Fr. Drake'. A rectangular panel has been cut out of the map at the right.

A legend placed by some 'huge rockes' reads: 'Here the riuer is taken out of the old riuer and caried 448 paces through mightie rockes which was thought unpossible to carrie water through.' Popular tradition asserts that Drake accomplished this engineering operation by magic, compelling a Dartmoor spring to follow his horse's tail into the town.

139 Preparations for the last voyage

Sir Francis Drake and Sir John Hawkins to Queen Elizabeth, Plymouth 13 August 1595.
MS 32 × 24 cm
Lent by the P.R.O. S.P. 12/253 no. 79 I

The fleet of twenty-seven ships assembled for the West Indian venture was divided into two autonomous squadrons, one headed by Drake in the 550-ton *Defiance*, the other by Hawkins in the 660-ton *Garland*. Both ships had been built in 1590 for the Queen. Other ships provided by the Queen for the expedition were the *Hope, Adventure, Foresight* and *Elizabeth Bonaventure*. She also contributed a large proportion of the costs of the expedition.

In the opening paragraph of this letter to the Queen, which they both signed, Drake and Hawkins wrote:

. . . we have no doupt but your majestie ys most assuredly confyrmyd in a good opynyon of our loyalltye, our fydellytye and areddynes to spend our lyves and abbyllytye to do your heighnes all dewtye and service to the uttermost of our powers, and ever with gods favour shalbe soo, and our indevour allwayes imployed for the good of our contry.

140 The last letter of Drake and Hawkins

Sir Francis Drake and Sir John Hawkins to the Lord Treasurer [William Cecil, Lord Burghley], 18 August 1595.
33 × 21 cm   *Harley MS 6997, f. 84*

The letter concludes 'so lokyng daylye for a good wynd, we Humbly take our leve, from plymothe, the 18 of August 1595'. It is signed by both Drake and Hawkins. They did not in fact leave Plymouth for another ten days.

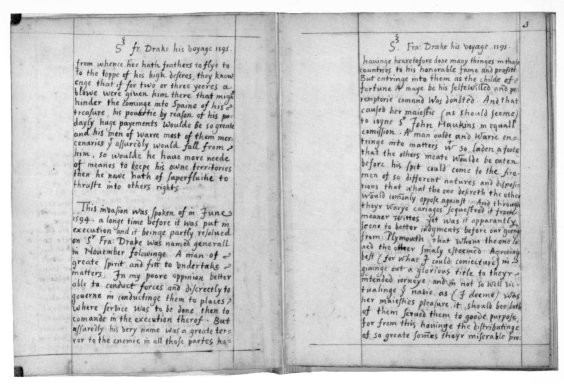

141 An appraisal of Drake and Hawkins

'Sir Fra. Drake his voyage 1595. By Tho. Maynarde.'
20 cm   *Additional MS 5209, ff.2b–3a*

This contemporary narrative of the voyage was written by Thomas Maynarde, who belonged to the Devonshire family of Maynarde, kinsmen of Drake. He was probably the second son of John Maynarde who held the manor of Sherford from Sir Francis and died in 1626. He described himself (f. 32b) as 'a younge seaman'. The folios illustrated include his character sketches of Drake and Hawkins. He wrote of Drake as:

A man of great spirit and fitt to undertake matters. In my poore oppinion better able to conduct forces and discreetly to gouerne in conductinge them to places where service was to be done then to comande in the execution thereof. But assuredly his very name was a greate terror to the enemie in all those partes hauing heeretofore done many thinges in those countries to his honorable fame and profitt. But entringe into them as the childe of fortune it maye be his selfewilled and peremptorie comand was doubted. And that caused her maiestie (as should seeme) to ioyne Sir John Haukins in equall comission. A man oulde and warie entringe into matters with so laden a foote that the others meate woulde be eaten before his spit could come to the fire. Men of so different natures and dispositions that what the one desireth the other would comonly oppose against. And through theyr warye cariages sequestred it from meaner wittes yet was it apparantly seene to better iudgments before our goenge from Plymouth that whom the one loued the other smaly esteemed. Agreeinge best (for what I could coniecture) in givinge out a glorious title to theyr intended iorneye and in not so well victualinge ye navie as (I deeme) was her maiesties pleasure it should bee.

142 Death of Sir John Hawkins

A Full Relation of another Voyage into the West Indies made by Sir Francis Drake ... Who set forth from Plimouth on the 28th of August 1595. London, Printed for Nicholas Bourne, 1652, pp. 50–51.
19 cm   *1045.e.22.(2)*

Hawkins wanted to sail direct to Puerto Rico but, after a quarrel, Drake persuaded him to attack Las Palmas in the Canaries *en route*. Their attack on Las Palmas was repulsed in late September 1595, and further time was lost by Drake's delaying in Guadeloupe and the Virgin Islands. Thus intelligence of Drake's presence and intentions was relayed to the Spaniards. Five frigates under Pedro Tello had been sent from Spain to retrieve 'tow mylloyns and a hallf of tresure' from a crippled galleon lying in San Juan harbour, and had reinforced the defences there by the time that Drake and Hawkins arrived on 12 November.

In the battle several English sailors were wounded by fire from the Spanish fortifications and '. . . the Stoole that Sir Francis Drake sat on was Struke from under him, as he was drinking a cup of Beere, yet by Gods providence he escaped . . .'. This 'relation' published in the seventeenth century records Hawkin's death on 12 November, though the cause is not specified. The Spaniards were later to put about the tale that he had died of grief occasioned by the ill-success of his endeavours against them.

By 16 November Drake was obliged to acknowledge defeat and sail away. The sacking of Panama now became his main objective.

143 Panama

'The voyage truely discoursed, made by sir Francis Drake, and sir Iohn Hawkins, chiefly pretended for some speciall seruice on the Islands and maine of the West Indies . . . in the yeere 1595.'
In: *The Third and Last Volvme of the Voyages, Navigations, Traffiques, and Discoueries of the English Nation . . . Collected by Richard Hakluyt*
London, 1600. p. 587.
30 cm   683.h.6

Drake sacked and destroyed Rio de la Hacha and Santa Marta after leaving San Juan in November; it was consequently 27 December before he came into Nombre de Dios.

In this account of Drake's 1595–6 voyage, in the second edition of his *Principall Navigations*, Hakluyt related how Drake took Nombre de Dios only to learn that 'Nothing was left in the towne of value' the valuables all having been hidden, so he burnt the town. On the 29th Sir Thomas Baskerville 'with 750 armed men, besides Chirurgians [*i.e.* surgeons] and prouand [*i.e.* provant] boyes, went for Panama', but returned on 2 January 'with his soldiers both weary and hungry, haueing marched more than halfe the way to the South Sea'. They had been caught in an ambush by the Spanish and suffered heavy losses. On 5 January they therefore set sail again in search of loot.

144 The death of Sir Francis Drake

The English Hero: or, Sir Francis Drake Reviv'd. Being a full Account of the Dangerous Voyages, Admirable Adventures, Notable Discoveries, and Magnanimous Atchievements of that Valiant and Renowned Commander . . . Recommended to the Imitation of all Heroick Spirits. By R.B. The fourth edition Inlarged. London, Printed for Nath. Crouch, 1695.
15 cm   304.a.26

At sea the crews were stricken by fever and delayed by bad weather. On 28 January 1596 Drake died from the 'bloody flux' (*i.e.* dysentery) in Nombre de Dios Bay.

This chap-book biography of Drake by R.B., that is Richard Burton, pseudonym of Nathaniel Crouch, is based on *Sir Francis Drake Reviv'd* of 1653, with additional material from elsewhere. The first edition appeared in 1687 but no copies of the second and third editions have been found (its popularity meant that it was frequently reprinted until 1762) and copies of this edition are rare. According to the *English Hero* and most other English accounts, for example, that given in *A Full Relation . . .*, 1652, Drake was buried at sea off Porto Bello:

> His body being put into a Coffin of Lead, was let down into the Sea, the Trumpets in doleful manner Ecchoing out their Lamentations for so great a Loss and all the Cannons in the Fleet were discharged, according to the Custom of all Sea-Funeral Obsequies.

145 Drake's death reported in Spain

A Libell of Spanish Lies . . . discoursing the fight in the West Indies, twixt the English Nauie . . . and a fleete of twentie saile of the king of Spaines, and of the death of Sir Francis Drake . . . With an answere briefely confuting the Spanish lies . . . written by Henrie Sauile Esquire, employed Captaine in one of her Maiesties Shippes . . . And also an Approbation of this discourse, by Sir Thomas Baskeruile, then Generall of the English fleete. London, Iohn Windet, 1596, p. 9.
19 cm   100.c.2

The author, Henry Savile, was Captain of the *Amity* while Baskerville (his supporter in print) had assumed supreme command of the Fleet as well as the land forces after the death of Drake.

Don Bernardino Delgadillo de Avellaneda had left Lisbon on 23 December 1595 with eight galleons and thirteen armed merchantmen to search out Drake but the two fleets did not meet until after his death. They engaged in battle off the Isle of Pines on 1 March 1596 and Baskerville had the better of the encounter. On the return voyage to England across the Atlantic the ships split up and the faster vessels reached home in April 1596.

Avellaneda reported in a letter ('Englished' and printed in this pamphlet) to 'Doctor Peter Flores, President of the contraction house for the Indies', written at Havana after he had been 'out sayled' by Baskerville, that at Carthagena he had '. . . had intelligence by an Indian, that Francis Drake dyed in Nombre de Dios, for verie griefe that hee had lost so many Barkes and men . . .'.

146 The will of Sir Francis Drake

Drake's Will, August 1595, with a codicil of 27
January 1596.
MS 39 cm

Lent by the P.R.O., PROB 11/vol. 87, f. 2d

Drake drew up his will because, in his own words, 'I am
. . . now called into action by her Maiestie wherein I am
to hazard my life aswell in the defence of Christes Gospell
as for the good of my Prince and Countrie . . .'. His

bequests included £40 for the poor people of Plymouth.
All his goods, furniture and 'housholdstuffe' in his
house at Buckland and leasehold properties in Plymouth
were left to his wife Elizabeth. The codicil was made on
the 27 January 1595/6, the day before his death, and
styles him 'Generall of her Maiesties Fleete now in
service for the West Indyes'. The will and codicil were
witnessed by Drake's companions, Charles Manners,
Thomas Webbs, Roger Langsford, George Watkins,
William Maynard and Jonas Bodenham who became

commander of the *Defiance* on the death of Drake. Bodenham had served under Drake in the *Revenge* and was his secretary in or before 1588.

147 The 'navigational journal' of the last voyage

An illustrated rutter of the voyage to the West Indies 1595–6, f. 13.
Ink on paper.
28 cm   *Lent by the Bibliothèque Nationale, Manuscrit Anglais 51*

On the last voyage someone, probably Drake, ensured that all the principal landfalls should be recorded in colour by a 'painter', such as had accompanied Drake on his circumnavigation. The resulting notebook of twenty-two folios is now preserved amongst other English manuscripts in the Bibliothèque Nationale in Paris. It may formerly have been in the collection of the Flemish diplomat, Henri-Florent Laurin de la Haye, whose portrait is pasted to the fly-leaf. The drawings or coastal profiles and descriptive texts include precise notes on the hydrography of the places visited, and in particular record the approaches to harbours, the setting of currents, the depth of water and the nature of the sea-bed.

On folio 13 the artist has included the following brief note on Drake's death: 'This Morninge when the discription notid or taken of this Lande beinge the 28 of Januarie 1595 [*i.e.* 1596 n.s.] beinge wedens daie in the morninge Sr Frauncis Dracke Died of the bludie flix [*i.e.* flux] righte of the Islande de Buena Ventura som 6 Leagues at see whom nou resteth with the Lorde.'

148 Death of Drake and Hawkins reported in England

William Stallenge to Sir Robert Cecil, Plymouth 25 April 1596.
MS 31 × 24 cm   *Lent by P.R.O. S.P. 12/257 no. 48*

In this letter Stallenge reported the return of the expedition and the deaths of Drake and Hawkins. He wrote: 'Thoughe I ame verie sorrie to write suche newes as I knowe wilbe verie unpleasing; yet I have thought it my dutie to advertice; on Fridaie laste there arived certen ships of Sir Frauncis Drake's Fleete at Famouth but himselff and Sir John Haukines with many other men of worth I understand are dead.'

149 In memory of Sir Francis Drake

A Broadside, 38 × 22 cm
Lent by the Society of Antiquaries

This is a unique copy of a Latin broadside published in memory of Drake. Drake's death on 28 January 1596 is given here in Old Style as 1595. This translation from the Latin is taken from E. M. Tenison *Elizabethan England* (vol. IX, p. 604).

In memory of
That most celebrated man Sir Francis Drake, Knight,
who of late on a naval expedition against his Country's
foes, died a victim of dysentery, on the 28th day of January in the year of Our Lord 1595.

He who in wars at sea such hazards underwent,
Through love of his own Country ever led;
Drake now at length the eternal shores hath reached
Of Peace, and hath for his reward eternal Peace.

To the Same
Thou that hast sailed the straits that lie beneath each Sun,
And those as well that may be traversed 'neath each Pole;
Oh Drake, for thee I heaven's high shores felicitate,
Though in thy death indeed our own lot I must mourn.

To the Same
Oh thou who wast the greatest Scourge of Spain, and who
To Philip's self wast source of fear and terror on the seas,
Oh Drake, thou passest; yet a hero still we have
In Essex who against our foes another Drake will be.

'To all who shall have safely kept and helped and augmented their Country, there is in Heaven a certain and assured place, where the blessed may enjoy everlasting life.' Cicero, in his Somnium Scipionis.

Happy thus the death of Francis Drake, in that whilst due to nature, it was yet for his Country that in chief it was rendered.

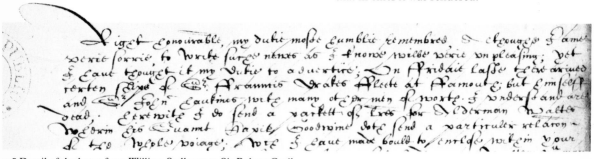

148 Detail of the letter from William Stallenge to Sir Robert Cecil.